The
RORY'S
STORIES

GUIDE to BEING IRISH

The
RORY'S
STORIES

GUIDE to BEING IRISH

Rory O'Connor

Gill Books

Gill Books
Hume Avenue
Park West
Dublin 12
www.gillbooks.ie

Gill Books is an imprint of M.H. Gill & Co.

© Rory O'Connor 2018
978 07171 8340 1

Illustrations by Jen Murphy
Copy-edited by Seirbhísí Leabhar
Proofread by Jane Rogers
Printed by ScandBook AB, Sweden

This book is typeset in Minion Pro 12/17 pt.

The paper used in this book comes from the wood pulp of
managed forests. For every tree felled, at least one tree is
planted, thereby renewing natural resources.

A CIP catalogue record for this book is available from the
British Library.

5 4 3 2

Contents

Rory O'Connor is a stand-up comedian and the mastermind behind the phenomenally successful social page Rory's Stories, one of the biggest social media pages in the country. Rory's first book, *The Rory's Stories Guide to the GAA*, was a bestseller.

Preface

So, after the success of my first book, *The Rory's Stories Guide to the GAA*, I very quickly decided to go at it again with a second. I have to say that, as much as I enjoyed writing about the great organisation that is the GAA, I definitely enjoyed writing this one more. Why? you ask. Simply because it has a few more real-life Rory's Stories in it!

When you read these stories you may think I made some of them up, but I can tell you here and now that what you're about to read is all legit. These disaster stories are what made me decide that I had to simply call my brand Rory's Stories. Also, because I was named after a high king of Ireland, was born on St Patrick's Day and love the GAA, Guinness and Luke Kelly, I feel I'm the perfect person to sum up the antics of us crazy Irish.

You'll find everything in this book, from an Irish wedding to an Irish wake, from your local nosy auld one to the bar-stool bullshitter in your local pub, and from your geek of a guard to your typical stag party. It's all ahead of you!

One word of warning: choose wisely where and when you read these stories. Reading them with hot coffee in your mouth during your lunch break is not wise – unless you want to land half your latte onto one of your work buddies!

Enjoy, folks.

The Irish Family

Irish Father

The Irish 'auld lad' is unique. He's as straight down the middle as you can get. My own father couldn't be any more of an auld lad if he tried: he grew up on a farm in the midlands, where he knew nothing but bacon and cabbage, farm life and the GAA. He loves old ballads and hates loud music, and he wouldn't watch a soccer match if ya paid him.

These auld lads always mean well, but they lose the rag easily. Whether it's showing you how to ride a bike or cut the grass for the first time, their patience wouldn't be great. Remember when they had to help you with your homework? What an ordeal! Your attention span was cat, your father trying to understand maths equations was worse, and it seemed to always end up in a row. It would often finish on a final line from your dad. 'Wait till your mother comes home to finish the rest of that with you.'

These are some traits you'll find in every Irish father:

- ☘ They get thick very easily and are hilarious when angry.

- ☘ If they come home from work to find that you got a bad note from school, you're automatically going to be a binman when you grow up.

- ☘ More than anything in life, they want you to play for the county.

- ☘ They can't sit still. Even if it's a pointless job they'll do it – anything to keep busy.

- ☘ They hate nothing more than the soaps on the telly. 'Coronation Street', 'Fair City', 'EastEnders' – drives them nuts!

Auld lads will make their mind up very easily, and if they don't like something they'll let you know. How many times have you tried to show them something on the internet, whether it's to point out a class footballer or to get them to watch a film? They're so stubborn it's unreal.

'Here, Da, wait till you see this. It's amazing.'

'G'wan, show it to me, there. It better not be long.'

Forty-five seconds in, no matter how exciting it is . . .

'Ah, that's bullshite.'

'Just watch it to the end.'

He will, and he won't be impressed by it whatsoever. 'Ah, sure that's not real. Load of bollox!'

The old-school Irish father knows nothing but hard work, an oversized dinner every evening and a few pints at the weekend. They're all great with their hands: no matter what's broken they'll fix it. You look at fathers these days (including myself), and we can barely change a tyre. I certainly wouldn't be the most DIY man in the world, so nine times out of ten I'd ring my father for general advice round the house. I'd be a bit simple about the day-to-day stuff, so my father's phone would be hopping a lot of the time, and he'd often be amazed at some of the things I'd ask him. I'll tell you a story that sums this up.

Rory's Story: Mousetrap

Most households in Ireland get visited by a mouse or two now and then. Well, only a year ago I was making a sup of tea in the kitchen when an unwanted guest sprinted across the floor and under the fridge. Now, ya know yourself that women wouldn't be the biggest fans of mice, so there was no chance I was telling my wife about what I'd just witnessed, or she'd be up, bags packed, and gone.

So I rang the auld lad and asked him if he had any mousetraps. He had, and he told me that melted chocolate on the mousetrap is your only man: the mice love it, and you'll have it caught overnight. Happy days.

So, that night, just after the wife went to bed, I melted the chocolate onto the trap and placed it beside the fridge. 'Enjoy your first nibble, pal, because it's lights out then.' So off to bed I went, satisfied that I'd see a dead mouse the following day.

The next morning I made sure I was out of bed and downstairs before the rest of the family. I walked into the kitchen, where I found no mouse but every last bit of the chocolate gone. How is that possible! I must be dealing with a genius, I thought to myself.

That night I did the same again, and I put even more chocolate on the trap – a mountain of it – so that, even if the mouse was good at the nibbling, it would eventually get carried away, and *snap!*

But, again, there was no sign of it in the morning, just a clean trap. For fuck's sake, I thought. This mouse is a wizard! So, like always, I rang my auld lad.

'Here, Da, are you sure this trap is working? I've set it the last two nights, loads of chocolate on it, and twice the little cute huar has eaten it and got away.'

'Take a photo of the trap and send it on to me.' So I did, and straight away he rings me back and says, 'Good man, Rory. Do me a favour there and stick your finger into the trap.'

'Why would I do that?'

'G'wan, there. Nothing will happen.'

I dutifully put my finger in and pressed it against the chocolate, and guess what happened? Absolutely nothing. The genius that I am wasn't setting the trap right, and the mouse was after putting on half a stone with all the chocolate I'd given it! I set it correctly then, and the little fella was brown bread the following morning.

Afterwards my father says to me, 'You know they usually come in threes, Rory?'

'You're joking me!' I say with a big, stupid, confused head on me. 'So is that where the story of the "Three Blind Mice" comes from?'

'I give up,' says he.

Moral of the story is: no matter what the situation is, the first person you ring is your father. Of course, he brought up that story during his speech at my wedding. Can ya blame him!

Irish Mammy

I think we can all agree that there's no better human being walking this planet than the Irish mammy. There's nothing they can't do or fix. An Irish mammy has many qualities; but, as you know, they can also be trying at times! My own mother couldn't be more on the money if she tried. She has all the Irish mammy traits.

- 🍀 She's a very keen woman to go to Mass.

- 🍀 She has her TV recordings bursting with programmes: 'Coronation Street', 'Room to Improve', 'A Place in the Sun', 'Countdown'.

- 🍀 She gawks out the window for any chance she can get to hang the clothes out to dry.

- 🍀 She uses the same teabag for as many as three cups of tea, and she's liable to put five baked beans and half a rasher back in the fridge after a big Sunday fry! Irish mothers simply don't waste *any* food!

My mother didn't care what I did as long as I went to school, got a good Leaving Cert, went to university and went on to become an accountant. (Well, that didn't go according to plan!) She wanted this so that she could tell her friends about it, like every mother. 'Oh, yes, he's studying accountancy in UCD.' Even if you were the wildest lad in the country, she'd always let on you're as good as gold.

Of course, when it comes to the Irish mammy, there are positives and negatives.

Positives

☘ No matter how old you are, she'll still make you tea and toast if you're under the weather.

☘ Mammy's dinners.

☘ She has an around-the-clock open laundry.

Negatives:

☘ She asks far too many questions.

☘ She doesn't get technology.

☘ She has a great knack for embarrassing you without even realising it.

If there's one thing Irish mothers are great at, it's being there for you when you really need her. No matter what you've done, she'll be there with the tea and toast. Here's a story that proves you can always rely on an Irish mammy.

Rory's Story: Too Many Cans

When I was about sixteen the music festival Witness (now called Oxegen) was on at the Fairyhouse Racecourse in Co. Meath. It was the place to be for a couple of days during the summer – pitch your tent, a bag of cans, your best mates and great music. Top-notch stuff. Being sixteen, I wasn't going to get permission from my parents, but we decided we had to go anyway. So one Saturday morning myself and the lads said, 'Fuck it, we're going.' We told our parents we were off at a GAA blitz for the day and wouldn't be home till late that evening. We stood outside the shops for as long as it took for someone to go in and buy our cans for us.

Once that was sorted we were on our way. Ashbourne (where I'm from) to the Fairyhouse Racecourse is about six miles, so it wasn't just a trot around the corner. We headed off through the fields, drinking cans and having the craic.

We eventually got there half cut and mad for the craic. None of us had a sniff of a ticket or a pass, so we had to jump over the fence. The adrenaline was pumping. We got Shane, the fastest lad in the gang, to jump over first, because once the security guards spotted him they'd chase him, and it'd open up for the slow lads like myself to make an entrance.

Off went Shane and, like that, all the security guards sprinted after him. Once they ran into the crowd we were over the fence, and in we went. I was the awkward lad in the gang, so I naturally twisted my ankle as I jumped down. But the few cans and the adrenaline weren't long in getting me off the ground and into the crowd.

The relief when we all made it in – it was some buzz being in there at sixteen years of age. I met a few of my cousins there and had one hell of a night.

All I remember is waking up the next morning in a random tent, having lost my phone. It was only a Nokia 3210, so not as worrying as losing your phone nowadays! I had no runners on me (I still have no idea where they went or how I managed to lose them), and I had only one sock on. Nightmare! The sun was beaming into the tent, and I could hear my older cousin on the phone talking to my father. 'No, he's okay, Joe. He's just gone to the toilet. I'll tell him to meet you in Ratoath in twenty minutes.'

My heart nearly sank. I'm dead, I thought to myself as I pulled myself out of the tent. I then copped that both my eyebrows had been half shaved off me by some little bollox. I looked a state and a half!

Before I could even take in the fresh air I puked, smelling cider off my breath. I'd had about twelve cans of Devil's Bit – horrific stuff – and would you believe that to this day I can't manage to hold down a bottle of cider? Many's the time on a lovely summer's day I'd attempt a large bottle of Bulmer's with loads of ice; but, no, two sups in and I get a flashback to that fateful morning.

I looked for my phone for all of forty seconds, and I just didn't care. I started to walk towards Ratoath, with my one sock on and my dodgy-looking eyebrows. It was the first time in my life I'd experienced a hangover, and I still think it was the worst I've ever had.

I eventually made it to Ratoath, where I found my dad waiting for me beside the church. I knew I was in the highest pile of shite imaginable.

Just before getting into the car I puked again beside the boot. Afterwards I crawled into the motor, and I still remember the look my auld lad gave me. But put yourself in his shoes: the last time he'd seen me I was heading out to a football tournament. Now, just twenty-four hours later, he's looking at a son who has half his eyebrows, sick on his T-shirt, no runners and one sock on, and he looks the face of death!

I said to him, 'Now, Da, please, before you take the head clean off me, can I just tell you that I have never felt so sick in my life, so please have mercy on me. Ground me for six weeks if you want. Just please let me be today. I'm suffering enough.'

Of course, he didn't listen to me, giving me one hell of a lecture. 'We thought you were dead', 'You're a disgrace to the family', 'You're a sixteen-year-old alcoholic' etc.

Sure what else could I do only sit there and be quiet? We had to pull in on the way home for me to get sick again. At this stage I was just heaving, and of course that's even worse. I was in a heap!

When we got to the house he parked the car and lectured me for another five minutes. It was torture. When we got inside my mam took one look at me and gave me a hug. Once my dad went out the back I begged her to let me have a shower and go to bed.

When I got into bed I heard footsteps coming up the stairs. I was full sure it was my auld lad with about a hundred forms of punishment on his mind. But, no, it was the mother, with a bottle of 7 Up, a cup of tea and the nicest toast I've ever had. 'Here, Rory, have that and get some sleep. Everything will be a bit better tomorrow. I'll calm your father down. He'll be okay. Chat to you later.' And, with that, she left the room.

That's why nothing will ever compare to the love of an Irish mammy!

Irish Grandparents

There's a big difference between modern grandparents and the grandparents of past days. Grandparents of the current generation are life-savers: they reared their own children during the hard times, and now, when they're meant to be enjoying their retirement, many of them end up half rearing their grandchildren as well. The kids are always landed at their doorstep whenever an occasion pops up.

'Mam, will you mind the kids Friday week? We have John and Emma's wedding, and we don't want to bring the kids with us. Ya know yourself . . .'

'Of course I will,' says Nana, and off the three young children go to wreck her house all day and night.

The kids love going to Nana and Grandad's, because they know they have them wrapped round their little fingers. The grandparents have done the hard graft with their own kids, so now they see the softer, lighter side of things with their grandchildren. They rarely refuse when the children ask them if they can take a trip over to the far side of the kitchen to have a peek in Nana's 'chocolate press'.

'Can I, Nana, can I? *Pleeeaase.*'

'All right. G'wan, then.'

When I was growing up, of course grandparents were very kind, but they were certainly not as willing to take the full bags and baggage as the modern grandparents are.

I had typical Irish grandparents when I was growing up. My father's mother passed away when I was only three months old. I believe she was a soldier of a woman, rearing twelve children but still having the time to make sure everything got done round the house. They don't make too many like that any more. My mother's father also passed away when I was young. He was a very honest man who always looked after his grandchildren. On Easter Sunday he would hide eggs on the farm – great fun! I actually put pen to paper for 'Rory's Stories' on the day of his anniversary (4 November), so he's deffo working his magic upstairs for me!

My grandfather on my father's side was your typical hard-working farmer. These men had too many grandchildren to entertain whenever all the cousins would get together on the farm. When we were young lads he would often say, 'Any time you see a bunch of chaps together, you know they're up to no good.' To be fair to him, he was right: we got up to all sorts of messing round the farm.

His list of credentials is as follows:

- ☘ He was never seen in public without a suit on, unless he was working on the farm.

- ☘ He loved listening to GAA matches on the wireless.

- ☘ He disliked all 'foreign' sports.

- ☘ 'The sign of a good man is how hard he is willing to work' was his motto. Not a bad one, to be fair!

- ☘ If there were spuds on the table he was still hungry.

My mother's mother was as perfect a granny as you could get. She ticked every box for a grandmother of that generation. These are her credentials:

- She was always dressed to impress, as if she was just going out to a wedding

- She *never* missed Mass, and the service would be her topic of conversation for the rest of the day. 'I thought Father Michael rushed it a bit after Communion. He must have been in a hurry to see the hurling.'

- Dinner was at one o clock, no ifs or buts. When you had dinner in my granny's house you had a full-on carvery.

- The 12 o'clock and 6 o'clock Angelus were the two times of day when you dared not speak.

- Porridge was ready for you every morning, and it was always the nicest porridge ever made.

☘ Tea was always served from a pot. Never would you see a loose teabag thrown into a cup with boiling water!

Because the world is much more hustle and bustle nowadays, grandparents are called on a lot more to help with children. They usually love it, though. Well, at least they let on they do, so we'll say nothing till we hear more.

'Don't you want to stay in Nana's house tonight, kids?'

'Yeah! Nana's, Nana's, Nana's!'

'See? I told you, Mam. Sure I'll pick them up early tomorrow [a lie]. Good luck!'

Irish Siblings

When you're growing up you might end up with a brother or sister, or sometimes both, whether you like it or not. I grew up with one sister, Carol. She's two years older than me. We were exactly like every brother and sister in the country: we absolutely killed each other at the best of times, and no one could push each other's buttons the way we could.

You see, because you know your siblings so well, you know exactly how to boil their blood. You know just what to say to hit the sweet spot that'll piss them off. Because I was two years younger I was the annoying little pest: she wasn't allowed do anything without me tagging along. I'll give you a perfect example.

Rory's Story: Sister Act

Carol was invited to a birthday party down the road by one of her friends from school – a party I wasn't invited to. I couldn't deal with this; I was raging. So what I did was call down to the house and knock on the front door. The mother answered.

'Hi, is Carol there? I'm her brother, Rory.'

'She is, Rory. Just one second.' And off inside she went to get Carol while I was standing at the door, scratching my legs (I had woeful bad eczema as a young lad).

Carol would finally appear with a party hat on. This pissed me off even more. 'What do ya want, Rory?'

'Mam said you've to come home. She wants you.'

'What does she want me for?'

'I don't know. She didn't say. She just said you've to come home.'

So off Carol went back inside, grumbling. She came back outside with her goody bag, and off we went back up the road. She kept asking me what she was wanted for. I kept my mouth shut, all the while keeping one eye on the Maltesers in her bag.

When we got home our mam answered the door. 'What are you dong home, Carol?'

'Rory said you wanted me.'

'I never said that.'

Carol flipped then and went for me.

When things calmed down, our mam said it was too late for Carol to go back to the party, so she had to stay at home. Carol was so angry that I ended up eating half her goody bag. Successful day's work for myself!

Such a little bollox, says you!

Sure what kind of a happy home is it unless siblings are fighting 90 per cent of the time?

The Auntie and Uncle Who Aren't Really Your Auntie and Uncle

Growing up, you'll always have friends of your parents who you're told from early doors are your auntie and uncle. 'Now, Rory, go with Uncle Tony there' or 'Rory, do what Auntie Jennifer tells you, okay?'

For as long as you can remember this pair have been your auntie and uncle. But when you get a bit older and start to figure life out, and to understand the family tree, you get a tad confused about it. You have a conversation with yourself while daydreaming in school one day, and the penny finally drops.

'If my name is O'Connor and their names are Morgan and Sutton, how does that make them my aunt and uncle? They've been lying to me this whole time!'

I've no idea why we don't just go with 'Tony' and 'Jennifer' from an early age. Putting 'Uncle' or 'Auntie' in front of their names makes absolutely no difference to a cheeky little two-year-old who's taking everything in like a sponge.

It's a tradition that has been going on for donkey's years, and it's unlikely to change. Maybe just chance leaving out the 'Auntie' or 'Uncle' next time and see how ya get on!

Growing Up in Ireland

90s Nostalgia

I grew up in the 1990s, and, without being biased, I believe it was the best decade to grow up in – no smartphones, no iPads, just fresh air and fun! Here's a few things that'll bring back memories if you grew up in the 90s:

- Sega Mega Drive (*Streets of Rage, Sonic the Hedgehog, Golden Axe*)
- Super Nintendo (Super Mario Bros, GoldenEye 007)
- Tip the can
- Cartoon Network ('Cow and Chicken', 'Johnny Bravo', 'Dexter's Laboratory')
- Nokia phones (3110, 3210)
- Dream Phone
- Freddy Krueger
- MTV music videos
- Spice Girls, Take That, Boyzone, B*Witched
- 'Buffy the Vampire Slayer', 'Sister Sister', 'Kenan & Kel', 'Inspector Gadget'

- Rollerblades (Fx1s, Rubberwheels)
- Tamagotchi
- 2Pac
- Ireland at the World Cup
- Premiership stickers, yoyos
- *Goosebumps*
- Callcards
- 'The Den', 'Teenage Mutant Ninja Turtles', 'Rugrats'.

When we weren't indoors playing *Streets of Rage* we were spending endless hours outside playing games like 'kerbs'. I'm not sure the kids of today still play it, but what a game it was. A one-on-one, head-to-head battle, and all you needed was a football and a road. You threw the ball against the kerb, and if you hit it you got ten points. If you caught the ball before it landed you got an extra ten. You then walked out half way across the road and threw the ball again. It was five points for the middle-of-the-road scores. This was risky, because the minute you missed it the other lad could hit you with the ball before you got back to your side and take your points. The real game-changer was when a car went by. If you threw it over the car and hit the kerb, that was it – game over – and you'd have the bragging rights till the next game. Savage craic.

'Premier League' was another popular game in my estate. You'd have eight or nine people playing, all lined out in your own square. If the ball landed in your square it could bounce once before you had to get it out. Whoever was in the 'Premiership square' (the best one) kicked the ball out. Usually they booted it down to the lower squares, where the lads like myself – the ones with two left fect – hung out. In all the years I played it I never reached even League 1 (third division), never mind the Premiership. A horrendous touch, one might say!

Then you had to go old school by playing 'nicknacks', in which you'd dare each other to knock on people's doors and run off. You were always dealing with different personalities behind the doors. You could hate one lad's knocker down all day long, and there was no fear of him opening the door. Then you had the harmless woman who was the easy target: she'd open the door every time, God love her. And you had the lad who'd chase after you down the road – we didn't knock too often there! We also had this auld wan who used to come out onto the road with two plates and roar into thin air, 'Next time I catch you knocking on my fucking door, this will be your heads,' and she'd smash the plates together before walking back inside. She'd often reappear three minutes later to clean up the mess. My God, we got some amount of banter out of her as we sneered and giggled behind a car.

'IRA' was another popular game, if not a very politically correct one. (The things you got away with in the 90s!) You'd split up into two teams, four or five people on each. Both teams would come up with a five-letter word, and each person would be given a letter. Once this was done everyone dispersed. Your job was not to give the other team members your letter, no matter what. When you were caught you could get the absolute shite beaten out of you to make you give up your letter. Some fellas would give up their letter after a flick to the ear, but other hardy huars would nearly have to have their arm broken for them to cough up their letter. It was madness, really, but we got great craic out of it. I think every one of us went home crying to our parents at least once, but of course you were out playing it the next day.

'Missions' was a similar game we loved. You'd go round estates, jumping over walls and running through gardens, trying not to get caught by a floodlight or a back-door light. Your adrenaline would be pumping all the time, as someone could hear movement in their garden and come out with a torch, and there you were hanging up in their tree. Game over! Guards called, mother phoned, and you grounded for two weeks!

If truth be told, we never had any badness in us: we were just a bunch of young lads acting the maggot. Long before your smartphones, this is how we spent our summer evenings, and I wouldn't change it for the world.

Primary School

Going to school in Ireland has changed a good deal in the past fifty years. How many times have you heard your father give you the old 'When I was your age we had to walk two miles to school every day and two miles back'? Back then, if you were sent home after getting a whack of the cane, your parents would ask what you did wrong!

When I was going to primary school in the 1990s everything was a lot simpler. Back then the school would have had one TV for the whole building, and, by God, everyone remembers that buzz of excitement when the teacher rolled in the telly with the big fat backside on it and put in a video cassette. Those were the glory days! We used to rock up to school an hour before classes began so we could play football in the yard. You'd run riot before the teachers had even landed on the school grounds!

There was some difference in what you could bring for your lunch back in them days. Nowadays kids aren't allowed any chocolate or sweets. We had a fella in our class whose father worked for Cadbury's, and this fella used to supply the whole class with chocolate. Most of us would be given a standard ham sandwich and a banana, which, as you know, used to end up squashed at the bottom of your bag. Or, if you were cute enough, you'd break off a bit of the banana, put it back into the tinfoil and throw the rest in the bin. That way your parents would think you ate most of it!

We learnt Irish two-thirds of the time, yet two-thirds of the classroom to this day can barely speak a word! I had a couple from Co. Kerry teach me in primary school, and they were both fluent. It was gas: you always knew they were arguing or unhappy about something whenever they'd have a full-blown conversation in Irish during the class. All of us would be just sitting there clueless, apart from one or two of the teachers' pets, who'd be trying their best to pick up a word or two to make sense of what they were saying. Meanwhile, myself and my buddies would be throwing crayons round the classroom.

If you went to primary school during the nineties, these will ring a few bells for you:

- Paring your pencil at the bin was for a bit of craic and a chat. Nine times out of ten your pencil was grand.

- 'An bhfuil cead agam dul go dtí an leithreas, más é do thoil é' was the one bit of Irish no one was long in learning.

- Whether or not you liked the GAA, you were doing it for PE.

- Aisling copybooks.

- *Ann and Barry* was how you learnt to read.

- School tours consisted of going to the local farm for the day.

- You covered your schoolbooks in leftover wallpaper so that everyone could know exactly what the inside of your house looked like.

- You had hairy trolls sitting on top of your pencil.

- *Busy at Maths* was how you learnt your sums.

- The teachers had chalk all over themselves all day long.

🍀 The excitement when your teacher was out sick and you got sent round in threes to the other classrooms, you and your two buddies causing havoc down at the back of fifth class.

🍀 Getting a duster thrown at you for misbehaving was a normal enough occurrence.

🍀 You knew when there was to be a fight in the yard, because a circle of kids would gather round two people, roaring, 'Scrap, scrap, scrap!' The fight stopped only when the teachers got wind of it.

Homework was usually the most difficult time in households: it often caused a miniature world war, especially if your father was left to do it with you. He wouldn't be long getting thick. 'Why do they make children's homework so difficult nowadays?' The few times my father had to do the homework with me, it was comical how stressed he would get while going through it. Now, I don't know about yours, but when my father gets angry I find him hilarious. He's much like Homer Simpson, so the more angry he gets, the more I nearly burst blood vessels in trying to keep a straight face.

'I'm warning you, Rory: don't have me catch you with that smirk on your face. You've been warned.'

Now, that's the worst thing a father can say to a giddy nine-year-old. I often had to let on that I needed to go to the toilet. I'd head in, lock the door and have convulsions laughing. Auld lads are comedy gold when they get thick!

Back then we wanted to get our homework done as soon as possible so we could get out into the street and start playing football and having fun. These days you have to get your homework done before you can have your iPad and sit on the couch!

Now, not everyone has gone on the hop from school. Most people would have more sense, but there's a few like myself who went on the mitch an odd day during school. I'll tell ya about one of the times I went on the hop and got caught red-handed.

Rory's Story: On the Hop

When I was finishing sixth class, coming towards the end of our primary school days, the weather was getting better, and things were winding down in the classroom. So myself and three of the lads decided we'd go on the mitch for the day. I'd been watching the film *Stand by Me* the previous weekend, and it looked like a great buzz: a few of your mates heading off into the wild for the day.

We all met half an hour before school started. We made sure we had smokes, sweets, a football and some food. Our plan was to head off to the fields for the day. We were naturally all shitting ourselves, knowing well that if we got caught we were in serious trouble; but that's what was great about the day – that nervous energy!

We headed up towards the fields, and by 11 o'clock we felt like we were gone two weeks. One of the lads was starting to crack, and he kept saying, 'What if we get caught? We'll be expelled and won't be allowed into secondary school. My dad'll kill me . . .'

'Stop, would ya! How will we get caught? Sure I'll write your note, and you'll write mine. Be grand . . .'

So we had the craic, messing around, playing football, smoking a few cigarettes.

The day we picked was the day the school were gone swimming. They'd swim between eleven and twelve, then there was a half-hour drive back. The coast would be clear at about noon. So just after noon myself and my friends Philly and Tom walked down past the school road towards Tom's house, because his mam and dad were away. We were going there to pick up some more food. We left our friend Simon in the fields to guard our schoolbags and that.

Just our luck, when we were walking down by the school, what was coming towards us only the bus from swimming. Would you fucking believe that! The one day swimming was finished early was the day we chose to go on the hop. So as the bus drove by, our teachers and the rest of our class looked out at us eejits standing there in shock. Talk about getting caught red-handed!

Our hearts dropped to the pits of our stomachs. 'Oh, fuck, lads. We're dead.'

Straight away we ran back up to the fields, and we couldn't blurt out to Simon quickly enough what had happened.

'Simo, Simo, we're bolloxed! The swimming bus drove by, and the teacher's seen us. What'll we do?'

'Well, I'm grand,' says Simon. 'Sure I wasn't with yous.'

'But sure they know we hang round together and that you aren't in today. They'll figure it out.'

'Nah, I won't be caught!'

Later that day we met a friend who was with the class, and he said that the teacher would talk to us the following day and that she knew Simon was with us.

So, messing, I said to Simon, 'Why don't ya look up the teacher's number in the phone book and ring her to tell her you weren't on the hop with us?'

Simon, the madman, thought this was a great idea and grabbed the phone book just as quick. I was trying my best not to laugh. Lo and behold, he found the teacher's number and rang her up!

'Hi, teacher, it's Simon here. Just to let you know, I wasn't on the hop today. I was sick in bed. I'll see you tomorrow.' And he hung up, delighted with himself.

I didn't sleep a wink that night, and I was too afraid to tell my parents. Off to school I went the following morning. Myself, Tom and Philly were put down the back of the class. Then who struts in, not a care in the world, only Simon, and just like that the teacher stands up and says, 'How dare you ring my house after school hours and lie to me about being sick, you blackguard.' Simon froze on the spot. Then the teacher says, 'The four of you get your bags and baggage and come with me to the principal's office.'

They phoned our parents, and we were suspended for three days. At home we were grounded for a solid two weeks. To be honest, it was worth every bit of punishment going just to see the head on Simon coming in that morning, happy as Larry, only to be brought crashing down to earth. Good times!

Secondary School

Secondary school is a daunting experience at first: new faces, more students, older children. You get split up from your primary school buddies, and you meet some new types of teacher.

The cool teacher

This teacher was up to the minute and treated you like an adult. If you gave them a bit of respect they'd do the same. They'd often have a laugh with you during classes and acknowledge you in the corridor when they'd pass you by. An all-round sound skin!

The scary teacher

No matter how much of a messer you were, you behaved during this forty-minute class! The minute you walked through the scary teacher's door it was army-camp time. You put your funny bone away for the duration: head down, don't make eye contact with anyone in case you get a fit of the giggles, and best of luck to you if you get the giggles during this class. Game over!

The sports-mad teacher

If you played sports this teacher was your best friend. If you got in trouble in their class they'd ask you to stay back for a few minutes. This wasn't to reprimand you: it was more along the lines of 'Well, how are you getting on with the county? Ya have a right solid panel there this year. You're doing the school very proud. Keep her lit!'

I had a teacher exactly like this in my secondary school, Ashbourne Community School. This was Mr Joe Gibney, a hero of a man and a massive GAA head. Once you were half decent at GAA he had your back. I was lucky enough to have had him as a year head for my final two years, and by God had I a safety net with him! No matter what messing you got up to he always bailed you out. No doubt everyone has had a teacher like Diamond Joe; but it's only after you leave school that you appreciate what kind of a character they really are.

The teacher you fancied

There was always one teacher you had a soft spot for during your secondary school days. Even if they taught you science you still looked forward to their class! You'd often cod yourself into thinking they liked ya as well; but, really,  you're just a kid in school with a crush. Ah, well, we can all dream!

The Characters in Every Class

When you moved from primary school to secondary school, chances are you just moved to a building next door that was run by the same priests or nuns. The kids you met on your first day in primary school could still be in your class when you were doing your Leaving Cert, so whether you were learning your times tables or trying to figure out what an oxbow lake was, you were likely to be sitting beside one of these characters.

The messer

This lad is just wired, constantly taking the piss out of himself or the other students. Never a dull moment when he's in the room! He can annoy ya at times, but it's good to have him to entertain ya in a boring environment. I might have fallen into this category myself!

The teacher's pet

You'll get away with nothing when this Harriet the Spy is around, always looking for a 'You're great' or a 'Well done' off the teacher. You tell these people nothing – a dangerous person to have in your company during lunchtime!

The weird guy

There's always one person who nobody can figure out. Ya can try to include him in the banter circle, but he just won't have any of it. He'll probably speak twenty-six words during his entire six years at the school – an easy target for the messer! He'll most likely come out of his shell at university. Hopefully.

The fella who loves himself

This chap thinks he's God's gift. Most likely he plays for the county and thinks he's the 'jock' of the school. In good shape, he smells good, looks good and, more than likely, is good at most things. But sure, like most Irish people, we might as well not like him, because he's popular!

The good-looking girl

This girl is probably the main reason that most of the boys aren't listening to what the teacher is saying half the time. They're in a daydream looking at this beauty. She might not be the soundest girl in the room, but sure who cares!

Teenage Discos

We've all been to a teenage disco. Most are held at GAA clubs or parish halls. It was the place to be – the buzz and excitement. I remember them like it was yesterday. Everyone would be chatting about it that Friday. The boys always sussed out the situation to see if the girl they fancied would be going – without letting on they cared, of course! At lunch their ear would be pinned to her conversation to see if they could get the nod that she'd be going that night. The sheer disappointment when they'd hear the words 'I can't go later, girls. I'm going to my cousin's for the weekend'!

You and the lads would try to sneak one can between the six of yous to drink before you'd go into the disco. Two sups each and you thought you were drunk and a great man.

The hard men would head up to the top of the dancefloor and stamp their authority on it. If you ever wanted a row you'd just head up there and start jostling someone. You wouldn't be long getting a slap! As the night wore on you'd be bopping away to tunes like 'Bobby Joe', 'Maniac 2000', 'Sandstorm' and 'Dancing in the Dark'.

When you fancied a girl you wanted to try and 'shift', 'meet' or 'be with' her (every part of the country has a different saying, but they all mean French kiss, I suppose!). Well, there was no fear of you walking up to her yourself and asking her to 'meet' you. Instead, you'd send over one of your buddies to ask her while you stood at the opposite side of the dancefloor and tried to look as cool as you possibly could. In the best case he'd come over and give you the good news. Then you'd walk over to her and, without even saying a word to each other, you'd just lob the head in! In the worst case she'd say no, then ask your friend if he'd shift her instead. He'd be straight in, no questions asked, and no thought of you. It's a double blow, that, but ya can't blame him. Sure you'd do the same yourself!

If ever you got too close to a girl while dancing, the torch would be shone down on top of you and you'd be told, 'Go on away.'

At the end of the night you'd leave and ask the lads, 'How many did you shift?' Of course, 99 per cent of them would lie and add one or two to their list, but there's always one member of the gang who wears his heart on his sleeve: he'd spend the whole night sitting with the first girl he kissed, caressing her hand and talking shite to her, thinking he was madly, deeply in love. He wouldn't be long letting go of her hand when he'd walk her outside and find her father sitting on the bonnet waiting for her!

The teenage discos are no doubt a lot more PG-rated now than they were when I went to them. Well, at least I hope they are, as I have a young daughter myself now, and it won't be long before I'm sitting on the bonnet of the car praying she walks out of the disco with her friends and not some random young lad!

Transition Year

Transition year in school is always a great option to take if you aren't in a rush to get out into the real world of college or, even worse, work! It's a little escape year between your Junior Cert and Leaving Cert. You've worked hard (well, kind of) for the first three years and are then handed the option to take an 'unofficial' year off the hard graft.

Two types of people do transition year. You have the folk whose parents believe they're too immature to continue on to fifth year and you have the geeks who've loved the first three years of school so much that they're over the moon to be given the chance to stay an extra year. To me, this second type is mind-blowing: from the moment I set foot in school I couldn't wait to get out of the place. But looking back now after having been in the real world, I'd give anything to go back to school, even just for a week: no hassle, just craic with your buddies.

I've often heard that transition year, or 'TY', as it was known, was a brilliant adventure, all the same. You got to head off on plenty of trips, you had laid-back teachers and you mixed with people and made a lot of new friends. One thing that would have put me off it was that you'd have spent the first three years with your close friends from primary school, but they'd move on to their final two years while you were left behind in the doss year. In fairness, it certainly is ideal if you're a bit young and not ready to head into your final two years. Everyone I know who completed the transition year says it was a great experience, and they certainly don't regret it!

*

Everyone remembers that moment during their first-year assembly when the principal advises the students to use their time in school wisely, because they'll be out the door and into the real world before they know it. You're sitting there, an eager twelve-year-old, praying that the principal is right and that you'll be finished your schooldays as soon as possible. The ironic thing is that you'll spend your schooldays dreaming of living in the 'real world', but when you're living in the real world you'll dream of going back to school. No worries, no bills, just craic and the odd bit of homework.

So if you're still at school my advice is – and I know it's easy to say now – don't wish your schooldays away: enjoy them. They don't be long going by, and the big, bad world is waiting round the corner for you!

College

They say your college years are the best of your life. I wish I could say that myself, but I lasted only seven weeks in the place. I did the Leaving Cert Applied, which left my 'college options' extremely limited, to say the least. Mind you, I have no regrets doing LCA: it was perfect for me, because I wasn't exactly what you'd call 'book smart' during my schooldays, and it allowed me to do a more hands-on Leaving Cert.

In September 2005 I attempted a sports and leisure management course at Coláiste Íde in Finglas. There wasn't as much pressure on me as on some folk, because my parents didn't have to fork out half their savings to put me through college, nor did they have to pay for my rent in digs, because I was living only twenty minutes away from the college. All too handy, says you!

I'd often watched films about the craic you'd have in college – these crazy parties and wild antics. Well, my days at Coláiste Íde weren't exactly what I imagined college would be like.

The college wasn't too big. In fact, it was tiny compared with most other colleges in the country. We had a small canteen where we hung out during breaks.

After no more than four days in the place I knew it wasn't for me. We were studying sports science, and this particular afternoon we were learning about anatomy and physiology. I sat there as the class went on trying silently to pronounce the words 'anatomy' and 'physiology'. My lips must have been moving and all, in a daydream up at the front of the class! I can only imagine what the teacher was thinking.

2:37. 'Right, guys, today we're going to study anatomy and physiology, so please turn to page seven . . .'

2:59. And here's me up the front of her class still mouthing *aaanaattttoommyyy* and *phyyysiiologgyyy* to myself. Run while you can, Rory boy!

From that moment I decided to just have the craic and enjoy myself. There was some amount of characters in the place, all as mad as each other. One fella who did do pretty well in the sports and leisure industry, to say the least, was none other than Dublin's teak-tough footballer Philly McMahon, the man behind one of the best books I've ever read, *The Choice*. I'd met Philly before college when I played against Ballymun Kickhams and Dublin at underage, so it was good to end up in his class. I can tell ya something for nothing: even though Philly takes no prisoners between the white lines, the fella could not be any more of a messer off the pitch. I had some great craic with him. We actually won a division 3 all-Ireland colleges medal during our time at Coláiste Íde. I played the first few rounds before I left the place, but I came back for the final as a 'banger'. Our team was classic: we had about five or six really good players, then just any auld Tom, Dick or Harry to make up the starting fifteen.

We used to put the number 15 on the back of one lad, a woeful sound chap, in every game and ask him to stand in the corner for the hour and try and hit a lad with a shoulder if possible. He used to arrive at every game in a pair of summer shorts, jet-black Dunnes Stores socks and a pair of them astro runners you'd buy below at the Fairyhouse Market. Two pairs for €25, and they'd throw a pair of socks in for good measure!

He also had a pair of glasses on him that were thick enough to survive a smack of a sledgehammer. 'I have to wear them, Rory. I can't see a bleedin' thing without them.' He reminded me of that little chap from the film *Little Giants* when his mother sent him into battle covered head to toe in bubble wrap – comical head on him!

It was great craic playing with Coláiste Íde, and even though Philly has since won five all-Irelands (at the time of writing) with Dublin, he's often told me that he's just as proud of his division 3 colleges medal with his Coláiste Íde bandits! That's right, Philly!

*

I'm slightly envious of you people who've done your four years of college. Off you went to your campus with a bag of clothes, a small notion of learning and a massive notion of having the craic.

A lot of the time your choice of course is influenced by your parents. 'I want you to have a good job now after your time in college. I'm not after working hard saving for your course only for you to go and have fun. Do you hear me?'

In all honesty, how many eighteen-year-olds know what they want to do with their lives? How many people do their four years, get their degree, spend a year in a job and then realise that this is all a load of bollox? Not for me, they say, and they head off down another path in life.

If only your parents really knew what goes on at college! I'll tell ya, this will give them a fair shock! If you're the standard college head

- you attend no more than two-thirds of your assigned lectures
- you put your lectures aside if it's a nice day
- your digs is an absolute bomb, littered with cans, crisps, left-over takeaways and stinking socks
- it's only now that you're a broke student that you taste the most horrific cheap cider
- you and your college friends bring 'pre-drinking' to a whole new level
- you'll never look at a Tuesday night the same way again: for those four years, Tuesday is your Saturday!

Let's be straight here: for a lot of young people their college days are the best of their lives and are an out-and-out session. Not many people can say that they have no regrets from those years, but sure if you can't go off the rails during your college days when can ya? Life starts to get a whole lot more serious when you're settled down in a job.

If you went to college in Dublin, well, it's safe to say that you'll be extremely familiar with that old haunt in Harcourt Street, the famous Copper Face Jacks. It's a place you try to avoid, but you always end up there on nights out.

Your Copper Face Jacks Experience

Where to even begin! Are you even *Irish* if you haven't had a messy night out in Coppers? It is, without doubt, the best known and most popular nightclub in the country. Nobody can ever figure out why or how. It's always wedged, it's extremely tough to get a drink and you need to be messy to enjoy it. Sure how many times have you had a few drinks and then walked into Coppers, only to realise very lively that you aren't on the same level of drunk as the people in there!

So many people complain about the place. How many times have you heard, during a night out, 'I don't care where we go, I'm just not going to Coppers again'? And sure where do you end up at three in the morning? Only at Harcourt Street's most famous son.

I found out not too long ago that they actually do food in there. So of course I had to test it. It was top notch, to be fair, but it was such a strange experience to be walking round the place in the middle of the day, sober as a judge. You think you know what the place looks like, but ya haven't a clue until you're inside in the cold light of day. You get flashbacks all right, but that's about the height of it.

The tradition of going to Flannery's till about 2 a.m. and then making your way up the lane towards the infamous Coppers queue is as common in Ireland as salt and vinegar on your chips.

The queue during a busy night is a nightmare, especially when the GAA season is in full flow. You'll have some country folk more excited about going to Coppers than about the match itself and a load of drunken people still in their county colours standing in the queue, trying to suss someone with a gold card to try and get them in ASAP. The Coppers gold card is a very valuable piece of kit, especially if you're a student up in Dublin. It's priceless, you might say!

Here's your typical night out in Coppers:

- ☘ There'll be at least one raw farmer drinking a pint of Smithwick's at 4 a.m.

- ☘ When you start to hear classic tunes from the Saw Doctors, Westlife and the Spice

Girls you realise it's nearly home time, so it's essential that you get in a few more Jägers. Not that you aren't already full to the gills!

🍀 You'll see a white-haired man standing at the front door. In case you don't know, that's the owner, Cathal Jackson. He's one man you make sure to be nice to. He's a very sound man, to be fair, and has time for everyone.

🍀 You'll witness at least one person getting kicked out and another getting sick at the side of the bar.

🍀 It's not just your ten pints and five vodkas: you did hear 'The Hills of Donegal' being played as many as ten times in the one night.

🍀 If you ever want to know what it feels like standing in the middle of a royal rumble, well, you'll experience it on the main dancefloor at 3:27 a.m.

🍀 You'll witness a free and single GAA county player in a pair of skinny jeans, a Ralph Lauren shirt buttoned up so that it's nearly choking him, and a pair of well-polished shoes, with no socks on, thinking he's the dog's bollox!

🍀 You'll find a couple of girls who, if you remember their names by the end of 'Wagon Wheel', will make sure you have the shift in the bag!

🍀 You'll spot at least one tourist drinking a pint of Guinness, wearing a backpack and having a Dublin tour map sticking out of his jacket pocket.

I think everyone has their own story of a mad night out in Coppers, and, of course, I have one of my own to tell.

Rory's Story: Cops and Coppers

Back in 2010 I lost a club championship quarter-final on the Sunday. Like most GAA heads, we went on the beer after, and a few of us joined the Monday club the next day as well. Like always, one thing leads to another, and, before I knew what was happening, I was at home in my bedroom, goosed, pulling my jeans up over my fat arse and telling my mother the usual. 'Don't worry, Ma, I'll still go into work tomorrow [lies!]. It's the end of the season, and the lads are heading into town. Sure I haven't had a drink in ages. GAA drink bans!'

So off we headed into town, and it wasn't long before we made our way into Coppers. It was quiet enough that night, and there was no queue, so it was grand. We went upstairs and started having the craic, but before I knew it was 4:30 a.m. and the whole place had cleared out, except for a few heads.

I went out to the smoking area, and a few of the Dublin team popped out for a bit of fresh air. They'd been beaten by Cork in the all-Ireland semi-final on the Sunday, so they were out on the end-of-year lash as well. I got chatting to them. 'Hard luck, lads,' blah, blah, blah. Meath had put five goals past them in that year's Leinster semi-final, so of course I brought that up! After a bit of slagging and shite talk we all agreed that it would be a great idea if I dressed up as a bouncer and threw Eoghan O'Gara out for being too drunk. O'Gara was new on the Dublin panel that year, so I suppose the lads just wanted to rip the piss out of him. Being mad as a brush, I agreed.

So one of the bouncers gave me all his gear – jacket, high-vis, earpiece, the lot – and I walked over to Eoghan and said, in a deep Russian accent, 'You must leave.' I still remember the look of shock on his face. I grabbed him by the arms and started to walk him towards the exit. If I'd known how strong a fella he was I'd have reconsidered what I was doing. Just as we were at the door, and with Eoghan trying to explain himself, out pop all the Dubs from behind a curtain, laughing and saying, 'You've been punked!' O'Gara just about took it all right. I offered to get him a drink straight away, which wasn't the hardest decision in the world, given that it was now a free bar! I drank there with a few of my mates till about seven in the morning with all the Dublin team, and the craic was ninety. We finally walked out into a bright Harcourt Street with everyone heading off to work. We looked well, I'm sure!

You just never know what kind of banter you'll have in Copper Face Jacks once you walk through the doors in the early hours of the morning.

The Driving Test

At some stage in your life, if you have any aspiration to drive, you'll be forced to sit your driving test. This is one of the most dreaded experiences in anyone's life.

The day of the test you're a bag of nerves. You rock up to the test centre, car as clean as a whistle, after you've made sure that all the empty bottles and crisp packets are well gone, and you've got a new air freshener – the lot. You've given yourself every possible chance of passing the test. The last thing you want is a grumpy auld bollox getting into your car and kicking empty cans out of his way as he sits in, a bang of stale cheese-and-onion crisps in the motor. It'd straight away put you on the back foot.

You're told during your lessons that the crucial thing is observation.

- Check your mirrors at all times.

- Use indicators when appropriate.

- Change gears accordingly.

- Don't keep your foot on the clutch.

- Keep both hands on the wheel at all times.

It isn't easy, but anyone will tell ya that the real obstacle is staying calm throughout. Nobody warns you about the lack of conversation in the car, the sheer awkwardness as your instructor ticks away at their boxes, and all the while you have no clue whether you're going well or not. The more he ticks the boxes with his clicking pen, the more you feel the beads of sweat trickling down the back of your neck!

There's a big disadvantage to doing your test in a busy town: you have people running all over the shop and cyclists getting in your way. Then you end up cutting out, so you have to restart the car, revving the absolute shite out of it to get it going again. At this stage you know already you've failed, and your interest in checking the mirrors and all the rest goes out the window. Get me back to the centre quick, says you.

Rory's Story: Failed with Flying Colours

I didn't have the easiest passage to claiming my full driving licence: it took me no fewer than four attempts to get it! For three of the attempts I'd argue the case that I got a raw deal, but certainly I can have no complaints about the second time. I had the mother and father of a howler!

They ask you a few questions about the rules of the road before you head out in the car. That was a disaster for me: I knew only three of the ten answers and guessed the other seven. These instructors are ice-cool. Even staring into their eyes to see if they flinch when you answer a question is no good: they're bulletproof.

I was a nervous wreck, and it didn't help that I had been on the beer for two days on a stag weekend, so I was already rattling with fear. Before we left the centre the instructor turned to me and says, 'Don't forget to put on your seatbelt.' What a start!

Then when we were out on the road he asked me to pull in, wait a few seconds, then pull off again. I was so wrapped up in checking my mirrors that I pulled back into the lane and forgot to turn on the indicator. The instructor looked down at his sheet straight away. Another black mark against my name!

I managed the three-point turn okay. Well, what I mean is that I didn't hit a kerb, which is an instant fail, but the arse of the car was fairly sticking out, all right. Towards the end of the test I was feeling that I'd made a hames of it, but because I didn't hit the kerb I felt I still had a bit of hope.

But that hope was soon thrown out the window by my next move. As we were driving down a busy, straight road my mind was all over the place. The instructor, to his credit, coughed a couple of times to draw my attention. But I didn't pay any heed: I just thought he had bit of a dose on him, so I continued driving. Then he says, 'Mr O' Connor, you're in the bus lane!' 'Oh, shite, sorry,' I said out loud. So that was deffo the final nail in the coffin.

On we headed back to the test centre. Usually you have to go in and sit down with them, and, after a few formalities, they give you the verdict. But I was in no humour for this. I just looked the instructor in the eye and said, 'We both know I failed with flying colours, so I'm just going to head off now. I'll apply again. All the best.' And off I went.

That was certainly one time when I went home to the mother and told her straight up that I had a complete nightmare and that I would be a named driver on her car for a few more weeks yet!

Theory test

A lot of folk, including myself, wouldn't be great at the theory of anything, and the driving theory test is no exception. You go into in this little telephone-box set-up and have forty questions to answer. The saving grace is that they're multiple-choice questions, so you have a one in four chance of hitting the jackpot. You have to get thirty-five or more right to seal the deal. Again, I had to have a few attempts at this before landing the badge!

Lessons

It's getting harder and harder to get any kind of licence. Back when I did the driving test you just got a lesson or two for your own benefit, but these days you need to do at least twelve before you can sit your driving test. There's nothing worse than when you're doing a lesson and you drive by a few of your mates, and you're cutting out to their jeers. 'G'wan, Schmacker, ya boy, ya!'

Working on a Building Site in Ireland

The building trade comes and goes in Ireland. It seems to be either a famine or a feast: when it's boom time there are buildings and houses being constructed everywhere you look.

A lot of young people who finish school and don't want to go to college look into doing apprenticeships in trades such as plumbing, electrical, brick-laying and carpentry.

You will meet all sorts of characters on a building site, and if you have worked on one yourself you will have had the misfortune of being a first-year apprentice: the lowest in the pecking order and bound to get a raw deal on the site.

In order to become a tradesman everyone needs to be an apprentice, and your job is to do everything that is asked of you, no matter what:

- Go to the shop every day to get lunch for the whole site – you could end up with forty chicken fillet rolls in your arms on the way back.

- At least once you can expect to be sent to the hardware store for rubber nails, a glass hammer or a long stand – the usual building site gags!

- The sweeping brush will become your best friend.

- You will be given a nickname that you won't be too happy about.

- Seventy per cent of the time you will be having the piss taken out of you without even realising it.

I was an apprentice electrician when I was younger and I was quite possibly the worst budding electrician of all time. I had big shaky hands, fingers like Mars bars and I was terrible at maths, so I wasn't exactly suited to the job! I only did it to keep the auld lad happy: 'Yeah, Da, I have my apprenticeship sorted. I start next Monday' – now go away and stop annoying me about a career!

I worked in an electrical factory that made panels for sites, which wasn't ideal experience heading into the second phase of my FÁS course. If truth be told, I should have jumped ship the day I was filling out the application forms and had to turn to a friend and ask under my breath, 'How do you spell electrician?'

My FÁS class was full of out and out messers, every one of us just mad to have the craic all day. All these fellas had spent the last 18 months on sites learning the trade. Most of them could wire sockets and lights, some could already wire a whole house – the real smart lads. Then there was me, who had spent the last 18 months making labels and sweeping floors. I barely even knew what 'earth' was. Lord Jaysus, I never sweated as much in my life as when we were told to wire an emersion! The stupid head on me standing there, scratching one ear, then the other, completely clueless as to what was going on! Thankfully there was a real sound fella beside me, and I was out straight with him: 'Here listen, pal, I haven't a notion what I'm at. Will ya give me a dig out?'

He could have easily ripped the piss out me in front of the class but he didn't. He helped and eventually, about two hours later when the rest of the class was done and dusted, my emersion was wired. Yeooow, ya boy ya!

I of course got the lowest marks in the class, but I was delighted with my achievement. From that day I knew that not in a million years was I going to be an electrician. Sure that was only the practical test and I had made a shambles of it, the theory end of things was another ball game altogether. I completely switched off in class when that was going on, and my foundation level maths in school didn't cut it!

I spent the remaining three months having pure craic. I went back to my company and my boss called me into his office: 'Rory, the results are back from FÁS and I'm afraid they're not good.'

I looked him straight in the eye (I would have known him well enough!) and said, 'Listen Mick, I think we both knew from the get go that there was zero chance of me becoming an electrician.' He agreed, we shook hands and I walked out. That was me back to square one and the auld lad on my case again about what I was going to do with my life.

The difference between Monday and Friday on a building site

One thing I did manage to learn on a building site was the routine of the week, and as you know there is some difference between a Monday and a Friday in any job – chalk and cheese – but I don't think any workplace sums up the contrast more than a building site.

Monday

Everyone is dragging themselves on site one by one. A lot of builders love a few pints so they will have a head on them after the weekend. That usually means something that seemed grand on Friday afternoon ('I'll get that done on Monday') is now a huge issue! If you want an argument, just walk into a building site canteen during the 10 o'clock break on a Monday morning and make eye contact with anyone.

You will find 80 per cent of the room eating their breakfast roles and reading 'Dear Deirdre' in the *Sun* newspaper. The boss will come in and let out a yelp, 'Mon lads, back at it! You're here 20 minutes already.'

You'll hear mumbles around the room, 'He's some hungry bollox that fella, not even finished my tea,' and off they will go with zero conversation, just straight back to work to get the day over and done with as quickly as possible. Monday is a gruelling day in the working world!

Friday

Ah, that good auld Friday feeling: the lads turning up for work a few minutes before they're due to start, taking their time with breaks, the kettle lashed on in the canteen, smiles on everyone's faces and hands being rubbed together with excitement.

It's tea time and the place is wedged with chicken fillet roles, the volume of chat is through the roof:

'Few pints this weekend, lad? Yeow!'

'Should be a great match. Myself and the young lad are gonna head in.'

'I believe the weather is to be good on Sunday. Might dust down the barbecue.'

The same boss comes into the canteen at the same time he did Monday, 20 minutes into the 10-minute break:

'Right men, back at it.'

There is no giving out about him on Fridays; everyone gets up without a bother.

'He is one sound foreman, isn't he lads? Bang on.'

Every young lad growing up in Ireland should experience a day on the building site. If you aren't into a bit of hard graft, it will make you put the head down in school and college, that's for sure!

Irish Occasions

Weddings

Stags and hen parties

Whenever you hear that your friend is getting married, after the whole 'Aw, congrats' you straight away think ahead to the stag or hen party – a chance to get away from reality for a weekend and blow off a bit of steam. The madness that happens on these weekends is unrivalled. There's pints at the crack of dawn, laughing and slagging, plenty of carry-on that stays on tour, and, of course, heart-to-hearts. Everyone stays together for the first part of the day, then it's everyone for themselves.

It's a great way to start a conversation outside the church after the wedding. 'Ah, good man, John. Haven't seen you since the stag.'

'Oh, don't even mention that word. It took me a solid week to get over that. Should be great craic today.'

Stag parties are one wild weekend. When you get older it's hard to imagine ever being as excited as you were on Christmas Eve when you were a child, but the evening before a stag party gives it a run for its money! For my own stag do about thirty of us went to Liverpool. There does be some craic in the airport when it's 7 a.m. and everyone is on the pints straight away, like a bunch of excited kids about to head off on a school tour.

A stag can always be broken down into three groups.

Ages 18 to 25. Full of life, they probably sleep a total of four hours all weekend. In bed at 6 a.m. on the Saturday morning and back in the pub by 10:30 a.m. Jägerbombs mid-morning is standard carry-on, and they can survive on breakfast, crisps and one burger each day. They're the life and soul of the weekend, and they have no clue what a hangover is! At the time, you think this will last for ever, but it's a very short window during which you're able for that madness. So if you're in this category, give it welly, because – trust me – them hangovers won't be long in keeping ya in the scratcher on the Saturday morning!

Ages 26 to 32. This is the age group in which you're in transition: you still aim to go as mad as you can, but it's a severe battle from start to finish. You hit the pints hard on the Friday, but you have to tell yourself to keep her lit. The body is giving in, and you'll often sly off to get some extra food on board, and you'll say nothing to anyone. You know deep down that you're just not able for the madness of a stag any more, but you power on with the young lads: brekkie and pub at 11 a.m. on the Saturday morning, letting on that you're good as new, but you're caving in inside. You come home from the stag on the Sunday evening and don't fully recover till the following Friday. You know that your two-day session days are coming to an end, but you're not willing to admit that just yet!

Age 32 plus. Whether you like it or not, you're part of the auld lads of the stag party now. It's a tough pill to swallow, but, one by one, everyone eventually ends up in this gang. You're at the stage now when you might not even qualify for the stag WhatsApp group any more, because you're too old to be seeing the kind of filth the younger generation are sending to the group!

It's a sad time. You don't even consider booking the early flight on the Friday morning any more: you work a half day on the Friday and get the later flight. When you land you're sensible and have dinner before joining the rest of the party, which is already upside-down drunk. You have a few pints with them and take in all the classic stories you were once telling yourself. You slip off about 2 a.m. when things are getting messy and stop off in the chipper on the way home. Yourself and another auld lad on the stag chat about the craic you used to have on these weekends.

The next morning you take a lie-on, as they don't come along too often. You ring the wife, who's dying to know about the weekend, but you tell her fuck-all! You walk round the town to avoid the drink for as long as you can, because you're gone past trying to be a hero. You know well that if you go for pints at eleven in the morning with the young lads you'll without question be asleep in bed with a tray of curry chips come eight that evening.

At this age you look forward to a stag not for the drinking but because it's a weekend away from the wife and kids and because you can catch up with fellas and hear a few good stories off the young lads – and wish you were twenty-one again!

Pre-marriage courses

A tradition that's still alive and well in Ireland is the dreaded pre-marriage course. Lasting a day and a half, it ensures that couples understand the meaning of love and marriage. Anyone who has ever done one will tell you they're pure awkward.

The priest will say, 'Now, I want you to gaze into the eyes of your partner for one minute, with a clear mind. Once that is done, I want you to write down what was going through your mind during this time – your love and affection for your soul partner.'

Most people will write down what the priest wants to hear:

☘ I will take care of you.

🍀 I will stand by you.

🍀 I will treat you well.

But what really goes through their mind for that minute is:

🍀 This is so awkward.

🍀 Don't laugh, *don't laugh.*

🍀 I wonder when lunch is.

🍀 This is some bullshite.

Some of the heads you see at the courses are classic. You're put into a few different groups for the exercises, and when I did my course myself and my wife got a good gang. All of us knew that this was just a bit of craic and that it had to be done, but there was this one couple who didn't exactly blend in. They took everything the priest said in earnest, and they were engrossed in everything. It was a bit weird, to be honest! For the part in which you look into each other's eyes, sure myself and my wife – we had been together twelve years and knew everything about each other – didn't know where to look.

All in all, the exercises are good craic, but they'll certainly test your patience, because the bulk of them could be done within half a day!

Venues and narrowing down your guest list

Picking a venue for the biggest day of your life can be tough! If truth be told, men are happy as long as the place is decent, but we have to let on that we're interested in the first three or four places just to keep our distance from the following question: 'Are you even interested in this marriage? You don't seem to care.' The truth is that we do care – we're just easy-going!

Both mothers of the couple will be well on top of picking the venue, and they'll have their say, as they always do. 'Now, are you sure this place is perfect? What if we get a very bad day? Will the guests be covered out on the balcony?'

Anyone who has got married will tell you the hassle it is sorting out the guest list. Here are some of the debates you'll have gone over a hundred times:

- 'We have to invite them. Sure they invited us to theirs!'

- 'Why would you invite him? Sure ya barely talk to him.' 'Ah, I know, but he's great craic.'

- 'Why do we have to invite them?' 'They're good friends of my parents!'

🍀 'Honest to God, I think we were better off having it abroad. At least whoever wants to go will be there.'

When you eventually send out your list you'll panic at least once when you meet someone you forgot to invite. You'll throw in the old classic 'Did you get the invitation?'

'No . . . When did you send it?'

'Ah, yours was probably in that batch that got lost in the post. Nightmare! Here, I'll drop another one round to your house this evening. How are you keeping, anyway?'

RSVPs

Waiting on your RSVPs to come back can be very stressful. It's a typical Irish thing: 'Ah, there's no need to send that back. Sure they know we're detto going.' Word of mouth is a dangerous thing in relation to wedding RSVPs. It can get the groom in a lot of bother, especially if a bunch of the lads tell him they'll be there and he quite simply can't remember who's who!

This causes many a row before the wedding, because herself is boiling with stress and you're trying to reassure her that everything will be grand. This is probably the worst thing you can say to a woman who's a couple of weeks out from getting married, because you'll get the 'I *am* calm' answer, which is always the answer they give you when they couldn't be any further away from calm. So my only advice is not to take 'yes' as word of mouth: get people to send a text to yourself or your partner. It will save a blazing row down the line!

*

Weddings aren't cheap these days: you need a good suit or dress, you have to book a hotel, and you need a few bob in drinking money. Men also need a nice pair of shoes to complement their slick suit. I ended up going to a good friend's wedding wearing a lovely suit but also a dirty pair of worn-out shoes, and here's why.

Rory's Story: Nice Pair of Brown Shoes

My shoe size is 14, so I don't have the luxury of walking into any shoe shop and just picking something up. There used to be a shop in Dublin called Heathers that facilitated the ogres of this world: they did up to size 20 or 21 (I wouldn't fancy meeting the man who wears size 21 shoes, or seeing what's hidden in his trousers!)

So the week before the wedding myself and three friends headed into town to get the shoes. We had planned to have lunch and a walk round the shops and that, so when we got off the bus in O'Connell Street one of them suggested that we go for 'a' pint. I said no, because I wanted to get the shoes first, and sure we could have food and a drink after.

But when we were walking down towards Heathers we passed a pub, and one of the lads said, 'Have you ever had a pint of Guinness in there?'

'No.'

'Ah, it's like mother's milk. Known as one of *the* pints in Dublin.'

'Really? Well, sure we – '

Before I finished my sentence one fella was half way in the door. ''Mon we'll pop in and have the one. The shoe shop is just down the road there. We can go down after.'

I didn't take too much convincing, so in we strolled.

To be fair, the pint was beautiful. We fairly sank the first one, and just like that another one was ordered, then another, then it was my round, so another round was down in front of us, and all of a sudden four of the nicest pints of porter were sculled. Then, as is usual when you have had four or more pints, the outlook completely changed.

'D'ya know what, lads? I don't really need new shoes. The ones I have at home are grand. I'll just polish them up for next weekend – be grand. Order in another round there.'

So about ten pints later we made the last bus home, half cut.

I woke up the next day and the mother asked me to show her my new shoes. Of course I told her they didn't have my size! The last thing I was going to do was tell her I drank the €100 I went into town with.

Fast forward a week later to the wedding, and while the prayers of the faithful were being read out I was kneeling and looking at my dirty brown shoes, which were worn to bits, telling myself how much of an eejit I was.

The moral: *never* go for the 'wan' before you have something to do, because, as we all know, there's no such thing as 'one' pint!

The big day

So after the pre-marriage course, the stag party, the RSVP panic and getting your clothes sorted out, the big day has finally arrived. Is there a better day out than an Irish wedding? It takes a while to get going, but once it does, my God, the craic is mighty!

This is how the day will pan out for you at an Irish wedding. You'll sneak in the back of the church just before the bride arrives. All the women will be commenting on each other's hair and dresses, and the lads will be giving each other that giddy look of knowing they're going on the lash for the day.

If it's not your own wedding you'll be bored during the Mass. Outside the church there'll be the usual chat. 'Weren't they blessed with the weather?' 'Doesn't she look beautiful!' and so on.

You'll arrive at the venue itching for a pint, and you'll check in and head up to your room. 'Jesus, nice view outside, eh?' you'll say as you throw your bag on the bed.

You'll then have a few pre-meal pints in the bar. This is arguably the most enjoyable part of the day, as you're having the chats and there's a giddiness in the air, and you know all the craic is ahead of ya!

You're called in for the meal then, and at this stage you're ready to eat a bull. You get stuck in to the free wine and enjoy your meal, and you hit the lull afterwards, in which you're only half arsed about being there, and you could do with a nap. Thankfully, this passes.

Up next are the speeches. Now, as you know, these can make or break the day. Irish people can be awful sneers. Who hasn't attended an Irish wedding at which the best man was so nervous that he got himself into a serious state and made a complete mess of the speech? This is dangerous territory, so play the safe card, I say!

After the speeches are over it's time to party. The band are on, and the first people up are that aunt and uncle who love a good jive at a wedding, so they own the dancefloor for the first ten or fifteen minutes while everyone else is hanging by the bar.

You always get asked the same questions by the aunts and uncles at every wedding. 'So how's the study going for your exam?' 'It's your final year, isn't it?' 'Are you still playing the hurling . . . ?'

After the band the DJ comes on, and the dancefloor becomes a jungle. This is when the lads pull up the trousers and tie the tie round their heads. I'd love to know who started this trend. Some drunk lad at a wedding must have just decided to tie his tie round his head, then got too hot and had to pull his trousers up to cool down, and without knowing it, he set a fashion trend for 2 a.m. at every Irish wedding!

When the DJ is finished playing his last 'one more tune, one more tune', the brave soldiers, who've been at it since 4 p.m., hit the residents' bar. The sing-songs begin, and you always have one person with a great voice who's plagued to sing flat out. Then you have the fella who thinks he's Luke Kelly and sings the same verse over and over! 'I've been a wild rover for many's the year, and I've spent all my money on whiskey and beer . . . I've been a wild rover for – '

It's about now that the drunken annual row among family members begins. 'You're ashamed of this family, aren't ya! G'wan, admit it!' This is when it gets very awkward and you finish off your last drink and head for the leaba.

Breakfast the next morning is not an ideal place to be if you know you had the one that's one too many the night before. You wander in and head straight for the cranberry juice, drinking as much as you can. Most hotels have shot glasses, so you're constantly refilling and holding up the queue!

Your shaky hands get you a full fry, and you try and spread the rock-hard butter on your toast. It's now that you begin to regret everything! But what craic an Irish wedding is, and these days, with most weddings being two-day sessions, you have to shake off the ropy head and go at it all over again. Great times!

Funerals

The wake

No-one gives the deceased a send-off like the Irish people. For the couple of days before the funeral the house is always packed. Friends and family come from all corners. It can sometimes be awkward, especially if you're not too well known to the family and you're paying your respects.

You walk into the house almost as if you've done something wrong, moving slowly through the hallway and nodding the head at whoever you make eye contact with. You make it to the kitchen and are straight away hit with a tray of sandwiches by the neighbour, who has every type of sambo in existence. 'There's some hot food out the back as well, if you're hungry. Don't be shy!' It's tense enough as it is, so the last thing you fancy doing is sitting down and tearing into a curry! After standing in the kitchen, sipping on your extremely strong cup of tea, with barely a word said you make your way towards the room in which the body is being waked.

You enter the room, panic, and end up shaking the hand of everyone in sight. 'I used to work with Paul. Terrible nice fella. Sorry for your loss.' You always get a quare look off some people, as much as to say, 'I'm not part of the family either. I'm here to pay my respects as well, buddy, but thanks anyway.'

The talk in the room is always tiptoe stuff. While you're in there you speak only when you're spoken to, you drink your tea as quick as you can, and you say your goodbyes and leave.

If you were close to the deceased you'll be in the house plenty in the coming days, drinking whiskey and many bottles of beer. A laugh is always gold in situations like this. It's always good seeing a character come into the room to tell a few stories. The bit of craic and a laugh is always good to help the family grieve.

An Irish funeral

How often have you heard, at 9 o'clock on the evening of an Irish funeral, 'Ah, sure isn't it the send-off he would have wanted?' A funeral in Ireland is a perfect example of our drinking culture. Funerals can often become an enormous session: everyone is advised by the priest to head back to the local hotel, GAA club or pub for 'light refreshments'. What he really means is 'If you want to go on the beer for the day, the family says you're more than welcome to!' At the pub you'll hear the following conversations.

'That was a lovely funeral, wasn't it?' I'm not sure how anything relating to a funeral can be lovely, but everyone knows what this means.

'She's in a better place now.' Nobody has a clue if she is or not, but we certainly hope so!

'Great turnout. Yeah, I've never seen the church as packed.' There could be only seventeen people in the church, but it's always packed whenever you ask about a funeral.

'Will ya have a pint? Ah, sure it would be rude not to have one for Mickey.' You might not have seen Mickey for thirty years, but you'll go on the beer after his funeral. Not much encouragement needed there!

'Have you work tomorrow?' 'I have, yeah, and I have to go in. Missed a good few days this year.

Ah, I'll be grand. I'll go in with a head on me!' You know well that as soon as you sup your first pint of a Tuesday afternoon at a funeral, you won't be going home any time soon. Being hungover at work is coming your way!

There's a great buzz and sense of togetherness as the evening wears on. The people closest to the deceased will come together, along with one or two others who love the session. A few stories will be told and songs will be sung. You're laughing one minute and crying the next. I think it's great how we handle the tough few days surrounding a funeral. There's a massive sense of community. Everyone is there for each other, and death can bring people closer together.

Cemetery Sunday

On cemetery Sunday the place is heaving with people. Everyone gathers in a big group to say a prayer for their deceased. When you were a child, even on warm, sunny days your mother had you dressed in trousers, a heavy shirt and a jacket as you stood there wobbling on the side of an old grave while the priest went through a decade of the Rosary!

All your aunts and uncles told you how big you were, after asking you the same questions over and over.

'How is school going?'

'What class are you in now?'

'Are you still playing the auld football?'

'God, aren't you the image of your father!'

The one person who does always be in flying form that Sunday is the local florist. Bejaysus, they clean up with all the fresh bunches being sold all week and placed on the graves. If you're clever you'll find a couple of young lads to sly off with down the back of the cemetery afterwards while the marathon of conversations is taking place. There you'll get up to a bit of mischief, pushing each other onto old graves, as has always been done! It's frowned on, but ten-year-olds who've been put through an hour of Mass will always need to let out a bit of madness!

Christening, First Communion, Confirmation

These three occasions are celebrated very similarly in Ireland. A Christening is a big day for the baby, who is welcomed into God's hands, but really it's a day for

Mammy and Daddy to go out and enjoy themselves. Both parents get the glad rags on. The father will stick on the suit, and the mother will go all out: make-up, fake tan, hair done, new dress – the lot.

Afterwards, you head back to a small function and have a few drinks, but the vital question – one that's sorted out even before the Christening cake is ordered – is who's going to mind the baby that night. It's generally one of the grandparents who gets the short straw, and they head off at about seven in the evening with the baba and a mountain of instructions and gear from the parents.

'Now, the bottles are here, the change of clothes is here, the nappies are here. Make sure to call me if you need anything.' What they mean is, unless the baba is unwell, don't even think of ringing me. I'm having a night off!

The father, who's outside having a quick fag with the lads, is carrying out his last duty of the day. The mother says, 'Mark, will you go down and put the travel cot into my mother's car, there.' 'Yep, no bother,' he answers as he flicks the fag away. 'Back in a few minutes, fellas.' Once the baby heads off, the craic can begin for the parents. Really it's the next day they'll need the babysitter for, as anyone with young kids will tell you! 'Oh, Jesus, me head. Please stop crying!'

First Communions and Confirmations are similar, although your First Communion is the first time in your life when you have a decent few bob. No pocket money here: this is the big time! The aunts and uncles give you a few bob, and without doubt it's the first time in your life you feel rich.

Most parents will make you set up a post office account with this money, which is the absolute last thing you want to do. If you're from a farming background you'll be advised to invest in a calf. There's a slag that always pops up in Ireland that, if you're tight with your money, you still haven't touched your First Communion money. I think we all know one or two people who fit this bill!

You have more of a say with your Confirmation money. Because you're eleven or twelve, your parents trust you to spend the money wisely. Maybe you buy one useless thing and put the rest into the credit union. I did the complete opposite with my Confirmation money.

I got, I think, £180 (the euro hadn't yet come in), which was a nice lump sum back then, and I bought a Nokia 5110 phone (the one with the game Snake on it), a gold chain and a poster of 2Pac. At that age I thought I was a gangster: sovereign rings on most of my fingers and a gold chain hanging over my T-shirt. 2Pac and Dr Dre were the main men back then.

Within two weeks I had lost my phone (I left it on the bus) and worn my chain during a match and got it ripped off me at some stage. I combed the pitch on my hands and knees for an hour after the match, but no sign of it. I had to tell my dad that I'd lost my chain only a week after losing my phone. As most fathers would, he got bull thick and said, 'All the hard-earned money that people gave you for your Confirmation, and what have you to show for it? Absolutely nothing but a poster of a gurrier on your wall up there!'

He was right, to be fair!

Twenty-First Birthdays

Twenty-one is an age you were always craving to reach. Eighteen was good, because you could legally drink (as if that stopped you before!), but when you hit twenty-one you feel that you're a 'proper' adult. You can get in anywhere, and you can even order a drink in America. You now see yourself as a grown-up. Well, kind of!

Your twenty-first is the big one. You plan well in advance, but you're worried that nobody will show up. You had put 9 o'clock on your invitations, but to everyone except the person who is twenty-one that really means 10. That first hour is one of the longest waits of your life.

The only people present in the room are you, your best friend, your immediate family and maybe an aunt and uncle, if you're lucky. The room is almost empty, the DJ is banging out the tunes, the crisps and peanuts are lonely on every table. You're a complete bag of nerves, checking your phone every seventy-eight seconds to see if anyone has texted you to say they're not coming. You turn to your best mate and ask, 'Where are the lads?'

'Ah, they're on the way. Just having a few bottles in Timmy's. Don't be panicking. Would ya like a shot?'

'I'd love one!'

Anyone who has ever had a twenty-first feels that pain, but come 11 o'clock you have a few drinks in you and you're having too much craic to know how many people turned up. As far you can see, the place is wedged. The twenty-one kisses will tell the story: if your brother or sister has to give you five of them it's far from ideal!

Going Out for a Meal

First dates

Going on a first date is always very awkward. Both of you are trying to be as nice as you can. You're always told to 'be yourself', but no chance of that happening on a first date! Usually the man tries to show that he's softly spoken and reserved, and the woman wants to seem easy-going and so tends to agree with most of what the man has to say. But, by Jaysus, that will soon change as the relationship develops! This is the kind of thing you can expect when you go for a meal on your first date:

- You'll both avoid the chicken wings as a starter – far too messy and risky for a first date. Barbecue and blue-cheese sauce all over your gob is the last thing you need when you're trying to impress.

- You'll only pick at your food. Even if you're starved you'll still stop yourself wolfing it down. Later on in the relationship, hands will be back and forth tasting each other's food – but no chance on the first date. Even if your date has the nicest food in the world and offers some to you, the answer will still be no. Unless you're *raw*, that is: then you'll clean her plate on the first date, and fair balls to ya!

🍀 No matter how bad the food is, you won't complain. Even if Irish people are handed a bowl of rats' tails we'll let on that it was lovely when asked by the waiter.

🍀 You'll have some sort of a disaster during the dinner. You'll either knock over a glass of wine or spill sauce on yourself. This is guaranteed to happen on a first date: Murphy's Law will pop up at one stage, so don't panic, and take it in your stride.

A meal with colleagues

Going out for a work meal is common in nearly every job. It's a good way to 'bond' with your colleagues. Most people are reserved in the work environment, so it's always good to get out as a team, enjoy a meal and not talk about work! You'll have a number of different characters out for the meal.

The dictator. The person who decides what kind of restaurant you go to and whether you should all get the early bird or not. A real busybody, this person does your head in!

The tight lad. There's nothing worse than a stinge. When this person is out for a work meal they'll be the first to take out the calculator at the end of the meal and make a show of the whole table. 'Now, listen, I only had a 7 Up, while Catherine had three glasses of wine, so we can't split the bill. That's unfair.' Would ya ever g'way ta fuck with yourself, ya tight huar, and split the bill – these are the thoughts of everyone at the table when the calculator is in full flow!

The dry arse. They don't talk in the office, so why would they talk at a meal? Whenever they do get involved in a conversation it's generally about work! You avoid this person when you all take your seats at the table. 'Ah, Jaysus, I'm not sitting beside John. He'll bore the hole off me talking about spreadsheets and emails.'

The hyper Harry. This person is generally the banter king. He loves the craic and will be buzzing at the table. He'll be the one trying to get everyone out on a session after. They might even land down with a round of shots to test the waters and see who's up for a bender. These heads are great company at the table.

'More wine, please – we work hard enough!'

Christmas

It's fair to say that Christmas, as the old song goes, is the most wonderful time of the year. Everyone's together for a few days, friends and family are home from overseas, and there's a great feeling in the air, especially after the 22nd of December.

Christmas cards

Christmas cards have always been a huge tradition in Ireland. In some houses you can barely move around the room with all the cards sitting and hanging everywhere and anywhere – nuisances! When you were a child you'd often have to help by licking and placing stamps on envelopes in early December. I could never get my head round the tradition. Just think about it for a minute: you have half the country stressing about sending dozens of cards to people they speak to regularly or to someone they haven't seen or heard from in donkey's years. And they'd all have the same message in them.

To the Maguires
Wishing you and your family a very merry

Christmas and a prosperous New Year.
From the Delaneys

Your mother could spend twenty minutes at the kitchen table on the 23rd worrying about a certain card she might not have received. 'I'm shocked that Mary Mullen never sent us a Christmas card this year. Would you say she's still upset after only getting an invitation to the afters of Pamela's wedding? I told you we should have invited her to the whole day. I might ring her to see if she's okay.'

'Mam, relax. I'm sure it'll arrive tomorrow.'

A text message will do in future, lads! Save ya writing dozens of cards!

Christmas Day

Every family in Ireland has pretty much the same Christmas Day routine. How young the children of the household are will determine what time the house comes alive on Christmas morning. If there's young kids it's the crack of dawn so they can see what Santa has brought.

Once the excitement of the presents is out of the way the mother starts to prepare the fry. The house is full of presents and wrapping paper, and you're already looking through the *RTE Guide* to see what films are on. You're always guaranteed a solid classic during breakfast. *Willy Wonka and the Chocolate Factory*, *Chitty Chitty Bang Bang* or *The Sound of Music* will be on the telly in the background as you mill your sausages.

After breakfast it's time for the only part of the day when the kids have to leave Santa's corner: they're dragged to Mass. The Christmas clothes are on, and off the family goes to the church. Just before you leave the house, the mother checks the turkey one last time to make sure it's on time for arrival for dinner that afternoon. The noise of the children at Mass is deafening. Fair play to the priest for trying to bring Christmas to life, but everyone really just wants to get their good deed out of the way and head back to the house to play with toys, eat sweets and watch TV.

There's a tradition of visiting before dinner, so either you visit relatives or they come to you. There's an exchange of presents, a 'You're looking lovely' and a quick drink. Then you're off back to your house to prepare for the feast.

Your mother's stress levels are by now hitting the roof. While everyone else is lying on the couch watching *Back to the Future*, she's in the kitchen running from the oven to the press, from the press to the boiling pots and from the boiling pots into the pantry, rushing to deliver the dinner on time, with zero help from the rest of the family!

After 'Is dinner nearly ready?' has been shouted at her ten times and she has finally answered, 'Dinner will be ready in five minutes,' you gradually come to understand that it won't be ready for at least another twenty minutes after those five minutes.

Then the time finally comes: you leave the can down, and on to the kitchen with you. There's so much food on the plate that you don't know where to start. There's a reason you have Christmas dinner only once a year: that's all the body is able for! Once all the food is gone and the crackers have been pulled, the paper-thin hats, which are too small for your head, are put on, and the cringey jokes are told. Then it's time to hit the couch for the food coma.

The food coma on Christmas Day is like no other: your poor body is in overdrive trying to digest everything. Amazingly, no matter how over-the-top full you are there's always room left to nibble on the Roses or Celebrations as you watch *Die Hard* with your eyes already closing, till eventually the whole family has a power nap, spread out all over the house.

When everyone has recovered from the feast it might be time to go visiting more relatives, or they arrive on your doorstep. More presents, more talking shite and more drink.

As the evening wears on, the famous ham and turkey sambos are prepared. Some might say these are even more enjoyable than the dinner itself. (Never tell your mother that!) They always go down a treat with a bit of mayo, mustard or brown sauce and a bag of crisps.

The family then attempts a few board games or charades, as you sup away on a few cans and a glass of wine. The older siblings might grab a few bottles of beer and head round to a friend's house while the rest of the family laze by the fire and watch another classic film.

It's a fantastic day to enjoy with family. Even still, some call it the most boring day of the year, which you can't argue with, in fairness. But I think it's a great day for recharging the batteries, eating loads, having a row with a sibling and making the most of quality time with the family.

*

Is there a more magical feeling than the one you got when, as a child, you burst open your living-room door at all hours of the morning and saw the Christmas tree surrounded by presents? If you close your eyes and conjure up that vision it'll still give you goosebumps. What a time to be alive! You're so excited that you can't contain yourself. You let out a massive roar and say, 'Santa came! Santa came!' Your mother and father will be making their way down, the poor auld lad half asleep. However groggy, he's expected to spend the morning putting together your train set or setting up your new games console on the telly.

I was a divil for not sleeping on Christmas Eve and was a pure nightmare for my parents: every twenty minutes I'd sneak into their bedroom and ask, 'Do you think Santa has come yet?'

'No, Rory, now back to bed or he won't ever come!'

Well, one year I took it a bit too far. Here's what happened.

Rory's Story: Santa Claus is Coming to Town

When I was about seven, like most gossoons I was in my prime for old St Nicholas. I couldn't wait for Christmas morning to come round. I used to *hound* the auld lad every day in December. 'Daaaa, would ya say the elves have my toys built by now?'

'Not yet, Rory. You have to keep being good right up to Christmas Day or they'll stop building yours and move on to the good boys' and girls' toys.'

'Okay, Dad!'

Well, this one year I'd requested the Sega Mega Drive (a serious computer altogether!) from the big red giant. Christmas Eve finally came round and I was wired. Not only was I unable to sleep that night but I was actually sitting up in bed rattling with excitement – not a hope of me sleeping!

As the minutes were creeping by I'd sneak into my big sister's room, pleading with her to come downstairs with me to see if Santa had arrived. 'Caaaarolllllll, will you come downstairs with me and see if Santa came?' '*No*, Rory, go back to bed.' (It was only later in life when I understood why she didn't want to rush down the stairs in hope of getting a glimpse of Rudolph and the lads.)

By 4 a.m. I couldn't take it any more. I'm going for it, I thought to myself. So I moved through the hall, taking each step as quietly as I could, and headed down to paradise. When I opened the door there were presents everywhere. One side of the room had a pile of presents and a note on top, *Rory*, and the other side had *Carol*. I started to rip mine open like a madman. Finally, the moment of truth: I found my Sega. 'Yeowww, ya rooster!'

When I'd finished opening all my presents I glanced over at my sister's pile, all the while thinking, Sure she doesn't care about Santa or her presents. I'll open one. She won't mind! Before long, one had turned into every one of her Jaysusin' presents. I then ran upstairs and, full of adrenaline, almost shook the life out of her in the bed. Within forty-seven seconds I'd told her every last detail of what she'd got from Santa, from her Dream Phone (the toy most wanted by the lassies – a huge surprise she wasn't expecting!) all the way down to the Spice Girls pencil case. Every last detail!

As you can imagine, this didn't go down too well. She let out an unmerciful yelp – the kind that would wake the dead. '*Dadddddyyyy!* Rory opened all my presents from Santy and told me what I got,' she said as she balled her eyes out.

I could hear the auld lad rattling the house getting out of the scratcher. I ran into my room and hid under the covers. He first calmed my sister down and then ordered me out to the hall to explain myself. 'Rory, come out here now! Rory, come out! Come on.'

I eventually came out looking like a mouse peeping out at a lump of cheese on a trap. The auld lad, standing in the hall in his finest dressing-gown, says, 'Well, Rory, what have you to say for yourself? Well, go on. Explain!'

I stood there sheepishly and said, in a very soft voice, 'I'm sorry, Da, but, ya see, I met Santa downstairs, and he said, because I was such a good boy this year, I could open a few of Carol's presents as well as mine. Not my fault!'

The father just stood there. As you can imagine, he was fairly taken aback by this pure genius of an answer. In fairness, he really had only one option and that was to accept my explanation. Otherwise he was going to have to tell me the truth about the greatest lie in the history of childhood. So no doubt he just stood there thinking, Such a comeback, ya little bollox, ya!

By God, I fluked that one!

The twelve pubs of Christmas

The twelve pubs of Christmas ... What an outrageous genius Big Darcy from Clonakilty must have been to have come up with this idea. Savage excuse altogether for getting a gang of your best pals gathered together and hitting the biggest town nearest to you and going on the pure rip. My memory of such days is of carnage from start to finish. Often ten, twenty or even thirty lunatics would head off into town dressed in Christmas jumpers of all sorts. I can guarantee you one thing: the full panel won't arrive home – not a chance.

How the day of pure and utter craic begins is that the gang head down the local dressed like absolute cabbages, each one of you as mad as the other, in great form.

'Well, Damo, you doing the twelve pubs?'

'I am, lad. Can't wait. Going to be class!'

You have the quick one in the local. 'Large bottle there, please,' then hop on the bus, in to wreck Baggot Street or whatever part of town is unlucky enough to be hosting the gathering.

The first pub is quiet enough – quick pint, then you're off. The second, third and fourth are pretty much the same, but by the fifth the lads are getting giddy. It's about then that one of the gargle-guzzlers shouts, 'Heeerrre, boysss, last one to neck their pint does a shot.'

The harmless chap of the group – the one who barely drinks but who promises all year that he'll do the twelve pubs in order to keep us off his case – this lad always gets stuck with the shot, and by the seventh pub the poor unfortunate wobbles out the door, asks someone for a spare fag, then staggers up the road. He reefs the phone out of his pocket and rings one of his best mates or his cousin from down the country. 'Just did the twelve pubs, lad. *Unreal* craic. Course I lasted the twelve. Sure I'm heading up to Coppers now with all the boys. Some women about the place.'

By now the gang are in the eighth pub. Even the 'decent drinkers' are goggle-eyed at this stage. One of the gang who doesn't smoke – he usually hates fags – gets cocky and has a smoke outside this pub. He inhales the John Player, barely coming up for air, when all of a sudden the nicotine gets a grip of him. He waddles into the jacks, stares in the mirror and says to himself, Be the Lord Jaysus, I am taaa-*wisted*. He shoulders some lad on the way out. 'Ya all right, Keith?' 'I'm grand – just making a call. Be back in a minute.' And sure he's nowhere to be seen for the rest of the night.

By this stage the gang are at the ninth pub, and the shit's starting to hit the fan. This is usually the pub where the 'mess' of the gang gets caught letting loose into the sink instead of into the piss-pot. 'Right, *out!*' shouts the bouncer. So that's the ninth pub written off.

As you head to pub number 10, a few of the more sensible fellas – I like to call them the 'better drinkers' – would say, 'Lads, Gerry, Marty and Tony are in an awful bundle. I reckon we leave them and leg it to a different pub!' *Gone!*

So then poor auld Gerry, Marty and Tony are left floating round the chipper, bolloxed drunk. Poor Gerry's in a bad way, pouring his heart out to the two lads. 'Did I ever tell you that yis are my best mates, lads. I'm telling you, yis are. I love yis.' Then good auld Gerry sticks the head back into the doner kebab for round 2. Tony pipes up then. 'Lads, town's a kip. I'm getting a taxi home. We'll have a few in Kelly's. Bit of craic . . .' Marty agrees, and eventually, with half a kebab on his face, so does Gerry.

So while the three stooges are half way home, the rest of the gang are split up all round Temple Bar getting fecked one by one out of each pub till one lad says, '*Foookkkk* Dublin. I'm getting a taxi home.' Usually two or three lads agree with him and bail into a taxi.

It's now 1 a.m., and the three or four die-hard drinkers of the gang are out of the game. One by one they find their way back to their hometown after being with women in the jacks, after getting into rows and after puking all over themselves in the alley beside Burger King.

When you wake up the next morning the first thing you say to yourself is God, Christ, I'm dying: thank feck that session happens only once a year!

Well, folks, that is, give or take, the average Joe's twelve pubs of Christmas.

The work Christmas party

Now this is a dangerous place to be. It's the one night of the work year when you let the hair down. (Well, some of you do!) It's generally a free bar or you're given drinks vouchers to enjoy a few beers on the company for all the hard work you've done in the past year. It's one hell of a banana skin if you're the very reserved person in work who goes mad with your friends at the weekend. Most of the company think you're nice and quiet, but what they don't know is that this is just your mask for work. In fact, you're wired and love the craic. Everyone has great stories to tell about their Christmas parties, and here's mine.

Rory's Story: Drinks Vouchers

A few years back I worked for an insurance company. The owner was a decent auld skin whenever I chatted to him. Now, for years this company had the absolute dog's bollox of Christmas parties. It was no-holds-barred stuff: free bar, free hotel room, slap-up meal – the works. As the recession kicked in, everyone had to tighten their belts, so, like all Christmas parties, ours had to be scaled back quite a bit. So this one year, instead of a free bar, we were promised five drinks vouchers each, which isn't so bad. Five pints of porter would have most people nice and smiley and mad for more!

On the Friday of the Christmas party we were all in great form in the office: tins of chocolates everywhere, loads of bags of crisps and good auld Mr MacGowan blasting out 'Fairytale of New York' on the radio. Great banter. As I sat at my desk, buzzing for the party, I spotted one of the big guns in the company dropping a load of envelopes on my boss's desk. Lovely, they must be the drinks vouchers, I says to myself. The boss started walking round the office handing them out, and when I got mine I opened it up and – I'm not joking you – they were raffle tickets with a dreadfully faded stamp on the back. No fancy printing or a date on them – nothing. They were just plain yellow tickets, the same you'd buy down below at your local wheel of fortune.

I thought to myself, Sure, Jaysus, this has be some sort of a joke. Anyone could just go to a pound shop, buy a booklet of these and use them at the work party to drink themselves into an early grave! And, just like that, my mind was running at a hundred miles an hour. So I rang a mate of mine (another cowboy) to see if he was on the same wavelength, and of course he was. So after work we headed to the pound shop and got two booklets, and off to the party with us.

We arrived at the hotel a short time later, and it was straight down with us to the bar for a few scoops to wet the tongue. We agreed that we wouldn't tell a soul about our idea: it was our little plan.

Later that evening we all got togged out in our formal wear, and by then the vouchers were being accepted at the bar. Now was our time to tempt fate. Being the cowboys we are, we gave another lad our tickets (which had no stamp) to test the water. 'Here, Johnny, take my tickets there to get us a round in. I've a few extra.'

So off went Johnny to the bar, where he ordered three fine pints of stout. The barwoman took the three vouchers off him and didn't bat an eyelid. As our guinea pig was heading back towards us with the three creamy pints, myself and my buddy looked at each other. 'We're made, lad. Let's go nuts!'

As we floored the pints into us we started to get cocky. Each time we went out to the smoking area we'd hand tickets out to people there. 'Here, I'm good mates with the gaffer, and he gave me a few extra vouchers. Have a few of mine.' As you can imagine, this went down very well with our colleagues. People thought we were the *boyyss*. I stood there with a JD in one hand a bummed cigarette in the other, handing out vouchers to one and all, like I was Arthur facken' Shelby.

Everyone was in serious form, and it was one of the best nights I've ever had. Then, come 3 a.m., I staggered up to the bar and ordered two vodkas with a dash of blackcurrant (it was all my stomach could handle at that stage!). As I had been doing all night I handed the barwoman a voucher, my sixty-eighth. But she said, 'We don't accept vouchers any more.'

'Why is that?' I muttered, in an awful drunken state.

'I'll tell ya why: just look over there at the till!'

So I looked over – struggling to focus my eyes, mind you – and there must have been two thousand tickets all over the place: in the till, on top of the till, under the till, on the floor – they were everywhere.

'Someone was acting the bollox with the vouchers, so we only accept cash now.'

'Jayyyysus, the cute huars, eh?' I says to her. I handed her a tenner and staggered back to my table.

I caught the attention of my partner in crime, who was on the dancefloor, in flying form, going mental to 'Summer of '69'. When he eventually staggered in my direction I says to him, 'Look out at that dancefloor, pal.' The place was absolutely on wheels – hopping, so it was. Everyone was in the form of their lives. I picked up my drinks, handed my buddy one and made a toast. 'You could go to college for years, but if you don't think outside the box the odd time, and have a bit of divilment in you, you'll go nowhere in this cruel world. Cheers, lad, and happy Christmas.'

December for the Irish people

Jaysus, it's a mad auld month, December, isn't it? The people you care about arrive home from every corner of the world – Sydney, Perth, London, Vancouver, New York, Dubai – to put the feet up, have a hot whiskey and chat about everything and anything. 'Told ya the Dubs would win Sam, Da!' Let's be honest, though: we do tend to spend a lot of this time down in the local, sculling pints and telling tales of years gone by, which is what makes us unique.

Now, don't get me wrong, there's also the sensible crowd among us – those who avoid the hangovers, the fear and the mistakes. The clever group, you might say! But there's the breed of us who enjoy the pints and the craic like there's no tomorrow. We mad eggs would generally spend two or three days each week in December on the beer. Now, I mean flat to the mat on the beer. Some of us could go four days if we're in great form, drunk and having the time of our life.

We fill our December days by soaking up every last bit of craic, thinking everything is pure gravy, saying to ourselves, 'Jaysus, ya can't bate Christmas. I love the pints – sure this is mighty craic. God, your man is sound, your wan is sound. I love life!' We drink the poor head off ourselves, using any auld excuse to go for pints.

'Did ya hear Ciarán's home from Oz?'

'You're messing!'

'Nope, the madman said nothing to anyone – just arrived in from Perth this morning. Nearly gave poor auld Betty a heart attack. I'll tell ya something: he's in great shape from working on the sites – big shiny brown head on him and all.'

'No way! Ah, sure we'll have to hit the town, so. Haven't seen Ciarán in years!'

Then there's the days around Christmas when you have absolutely no reason on earth to drink porter. One of the gang will say, 'Ah, feck this, lads. It's Christmas. I'm going down to Dicey's for a scoop. Sure I'm off it for good in January!' This craic would usually last for three days, till your body hits a wall. 'Nah, lads, I'm in an awful heap. *Die Hard 2* is on da box tonight, so I'm staying low – get in an auld pizza and recharge the batteries for Stephen's Day!'

Unfortunately, though, what goes up must come down. You spend the next few days feeling down and out, sitting on the couch bored senseless and scratching your arse. Not only that, you'll be rooting through the box of Celebrations, and, sure enough, the day you're having, there'll be only auld squashed

Bounties left in the shagging tin. 'Ah, for Jaysus' sake, Ma! Who ate all the sweets?'

At about that time your mind will want to have a chat with you. 'I really am a useless huar. I need to sort my life out and cop on. I have no money. That drink is no good for me!' What gets you through this downtime is knowing that Kevin from Kilbeggan is in the same boat: pure raging with his carry-on over the past few days. As is Liam from Letterkenny, Brendan from Ballymun and Big Tim from Tullamore.

Ah, but ya see, folks, then there's the one day, smack bang in the middle of this hectic schedule, when you're in a solid state of mind. You have no drink in the system and you're saying to yourself, 'Ah, sure fuck it. I'm an ordinary man. I'll drive on with life in the new year and hopefully get a bit of luck down the road. I'll be grand. Sure there's plenty like me.'

On that very same day, some time in the afternoon when you're half way through *Ghostbusters*, you'll get the famous 'goo' for a few pints and a bit of craic with the lads. So you slip on the drinking boots and off out the door with you! ''Mon, ya right, Bosco? We go for a few pints. Sure it's Christmas!'

I'm happy with this hectic up-and-down routine for the festive season. So be sure to realise, when you feel that nothing is going right, that there are plenty more people in the same boat. So all I'll say is just banish the demons during the sober days, because the absolute craic you'll have with friends and family during those two or three days of the week spent inhaling porter is what Christmas is all about.

Summer in Ireland

Is there such a thing as an Irish summer? Back when I was growing up in the 1990s we certainly did have proper summers, when it went at least a week without rain, but now we don't often seem to be as lucky! That's until the summer of 2018 came along, the best summer I can remember. I think we went about five or six weeks without rain, with everyone probably afraid they were finally getting sick of the hot weather. To be fair, trying to sleep at night was a nightmare, but I wasn't complaining; being able to wear a pair of shorts for 40 odd days straight was mighty. But will we ever see another summer like it in Ireland? It's hard to know. As a nation, are we even able for hot summers? We aren't cut out for it, as my mother would say. We pray and pray for nice weather, and then, when it does come, within a day or two you hear all the auld biddies at the supermarket moaning,

'Jesus, it's very hot, isn't it? I'm struggling to sleep at night these days. A bit of rain would be nice!'

A bit of *rain* would be nice? Are you mad or what! Well, in fairness, the poor farmers were under pressure because of the crazy 2018 summer heat – they wanted rain more than a hot dinner! And when we do get a few savage days in a row the country struggles to function. Everyone is wired and can't think of anything but a barbecue and a few bottles of cold beer out in the back garden. Imagine if we did get a whole summer of sunshine! With the summer we had in 2018 I'd say that butchers are millionaires and off-licence owners are billionaires!

Because we've been so starved of sunshine, all it takes is barely 18 degrees and we lose all sense of cop-on and think we're in the Caribbean! The lads will have the tops off down in the local field, supping on the few cans; the mothers will be out in the back with barely a stitch on, covered in baby oil and craving that tan; and the smell of freshly cut grass will have the hay-fever heads hiding under the kitchen table!

Summers as I remember them were special: no phones, no hassle and more freedom. The pitch-and-putt course in Ashbourne was the place to be. I'd get my pitcher and putter, one pound in my arse pocket, and off I went. I'd be gone twelve hours a day, not a word out of me. The pound did me for some

TK and crisps, and I'd go home when I got hungry. It was out on the streets during the summer that we had the most craic, playing everything from kerbs and nick-nacks to premier league. Simple life!

An Irish barbecue

Whenever we do get a nice day during the summer, a barbecue out the back is always in order. Here's the exact course of events:

- Your auld lad pulls the dusty barbecue out from the shed. 'Can someone give me a hand with this, please, instead of ye just standing there looking at me?'

- He takes for ever in getting it up and running. 'I think this has had its day, lads. Fuck it, anyway!'

- He makes the trip to the butcher's for your burgers, sausages and, if you're feeling rich, steak. 'Any special offers on?'

- A bag of cans is a must. 'Sure ya can't have a barbecue without a few cold ones, Ma. Be like you going to Mass and not blessing yourself!'

- The men always insist on doing the cooking, even though they burn pretty much everything. 'That's the way sausages are supposed to look! You can never be too careful with meat . . .'

☘ The 'salad' consists of coleslaw, cheese and whatever else looked a bit like salad in the fridge. 'Will I put on some frozen peas or is what we have all right?'

It nearly always begins to rain just when you have the food nearly cooked, and you all end up eating inside with your T-shirt and shorts on, looking like a bunch of gobshites. 'Would you believe that! The forecast said the showers wouldn't hit here till late tonight. Fucking unbelievable this country is, I swear to God!'

My mother, having been reared on a farm with plenty of mouths to feed, would be liable to leave one burnt sausage and a quarter piece of chicken breast in the fridge for up to three days after the barbecue. Irish mothers don't like wasting food, that's for sure!

The Irish abroad

As we all know, nobody loves a sunny holiday like the Irish. And why wouldn't we? Look at the weather we have to deal with all year round! We're unique when it comes to going on holidays. Every Irish lad, when he's packing, will include the following:

- ☘ Penney's socks
- ☘ Penney's boxers
- ☘ Penney's T-shirts
- ☘ Penney's shorts
- ☘ his county jersey
- ☘ Penny's runners
- ☘ his Bart Simpson towel
- ☘ Penney's togs
- ☘ a cheap sun cream
- ☘ Penney's flip-flops.

Irish people will get to the airport with more time to spare than most other people. With a big, giddy head on you, you walk into the airport wearing your new clothes, especially runners (you can't go to the airport without wearing a new pair). You have to get the boring security and check-in out of the way before you can really start your holiday. Going through security is always an intimidating time: even though you know you're a good skin, you still feel like a criminal when you walk through the scanner. Your heart skips a beat as you walk through, and you're asked to stand to the side as they move their handheld wands up and down your body. You think, Has someone stuffed a heap of drugs into my pockets when I wasn't looking? Oh, fuck!

You feel the relief every time they motion you on to collect your bag, wallet, keys, phone and belt. You struggle to get the belt back on, because your hands are shaking. You still feel like you're being watched!

With that task out of the way, you head up to the food area. It might be only six in the morning, but a pint is an essential with your breakfast. Even if you don't drink, you still do it so you can post a photo of it on social media, letting the world know that you're going on holiday. Your post will say: 'Finally, it's holiday time. Tenerife, here we come!' But what you really want to write is: 'As you can clearly see, I'm off on my holidays, so I'm posting a picture of this pint to piss you off. I know that you'll be getting up for work shortly and that this picture will make you mad with envy. Enjoy work and the weeks of shitty weather ahead of you!'

The boarding gate has been announced as open, so, like most Irish people, you panic, drop everything and head for the gate. Even though there's a massive queue, you still feel the need to stand there like an eejit instead of sitting down and relaxing.

A couple of overpriced small cans and a box of crisps on the flight and you're happy as Larry. When you need to use the toilet there'll always be three people in front of you. This can be awkward as you all nod at each other and then aimlessly look round till it's your time to use the toilet. You squeeze yourself in to the tiny room and let loose. You're always half asleep on a plane, so you're never prepared for how loud the sound is when you flush. Smart folk will put the fingers in the ears, but most people are unprepared and almost have a heart attack. 'Jaysus, the noise off that!'

After landing you feel the blast of heat as you step off the plane. Then it's off to collect your bags, grab a taxi and head for your resort. Already the zippy is tied round your waist and the cotton bottoms are rolled up. 'The heat, lads!' You get to your accommodation, check in, throw the bag in and root out the shorts. You're eager to head for the pool, but if she's with you the Irish mammy has to find the safe in the room so she can put the passports and valuables in it. Then she'll have to wander off to find a supermarket so she can get the essentials: milk, bread, yoghurt, water, biscuits and fruit.

The teabags will already have been packed in the suitcase, because, no matter if it's 40 degrees, the mother needs her sup of tea out on the balcony as her hair is drying in the evenings. Most people would love a nice chilled beer or a glass of juice, but the Irish mammy needs her cup of scald to keep her sane!

It's very easy to spot an Irishman on holidays. If they tick these boxes you have a 100 per cent Irishman in the sun:

- He'll be wearing the county jersey. This is so any other Irish people in the area will know what county he's from and that he's proud of that fact.

- He'll be wearing socks and sandals. Even though the feet will be sweating, he won't care. Socks and sandals is a comfort. And these are no ankle socks either: the socks have to be thick ones and pulled half way up the shins.

- He'll have a bumbag round the waist so everyone can know he's a tourist. Everything valuable will be wrapped round his waist, making it nearly impossible for local thieves to rob him. 'You can never be too careful, Kathleen. You're dealing with a different breed of thieves over here: these lads are cute huars, and they'll do you without you even having a clue!'

🍀 He'll be wearing golf shorts pulled up to his belly button.

🍀 He'll have peaked cap pulled down over his eyes and a pair of stupid-looking sunglasses on top of the cap.

'The early bird catches the worm'

I don't think any scenario suits this phrase better than the race to get a poolside lounger on holiday. First come, first served! It's always the mother who gets there first. She rustles about the hotel apartment at all hours of the morning while you're half asleep, and you ask her, 'Where you going, Ma?' She answers, 'I'm going down to put a few towels on the beds beside the pool. They'll be gone in the next ten minutes, and we'll have to lie on the prickly grass if I don't.'

Ah, sure she's right. There'll be a crowd of eager beavers patiently waiting behind the ropes for the pool attendant to open the pool and declare a free-for-all. Everyone runs to grab the poolside beds and throw down the towels. Once a towel is on a bed it's a mortal sin to sit there. I once witnessed someone pick up a couple of towels and put their own down, which left these people on the bed down at the back. Bejaysus, there was nearly war over it. This is just something you don't do on holidays. Either you get up when the birds are singing so you can claim your sunbed or you sit down at the back for the day. The choice is yours!

The beach

When you're lying on the beach observing everything around you, you get a giggle when you spot an Irish family ploughing along the beach looking for a space. The eldest child will be out in front trying to find a free area in which to camp for the day, and the mother will be behind him roaring at the husband to hurry up, even though the poor man is carrying everything: the towels, the beach balls, the bucket and spade, the homemade sambos – the lot – not to mention that he's dehydrating by the second after the ten pints of San Miguel the night before. On top of that, he has the two younger kids asking him if they can bury him in the sand. The man is under serious pressure. 'Jesus Christ, Aoife, I'm going as fast as I can!'

When Irish people cross each other's paths on holidays it's always the same conversation. You hear an Irish accent by the bar and begin a conversation.

'Well, how's things? Some weather, isn't it!'

'Ah, stop, 'tis unreal. I got burnt the first day, so I have to wear a T-shirt since. Not ideal, but sure what can ya do!'

'Yeah, God, the sun is lethal. Where are you from?'

'Oh, I'm from Ireland' – as if the Kilkenny jersey and the milky legs didn't give it away.

'Are you here for long?'

'We've been here ten days already, another four to go. The thoughts of going home . . . Though I've heard that the weather is very good at home at the minute. I was on to my mother last night.'

'So I hear. I was raging when I heard about the weather. Typical: you pay good money to go away for a bit of sun, and the week you head off Ireland is having a heatwave!'

'I know! It's always the way, isn't it? Did you find the Irish bar down the road? They're showing all the GAA matches. We were in there last Sunday for the Kilkenny and Cork game. Place was packed, great auld buzz in the place!'

'Ah, mighty Galway are playing this Sunday. Delighted now I'll be able to watch it. We're going well at the minute!'

'Did you find any markets yet? The wife is mad to do some shopping. Ya know yourself!'

'Yeah, there's a good one about twelve miles away, and it's only about seven euro in a taxi. Great bargains: we got plenty of presents there.'

'Ah, that's the shot. We'll check that out. Right, sure enjoy the rest of your holiday. We might see yas around for a drink!'

There's a great chance you'll meet them that night, and by 2 a.m. you'll be telling them your life story. That's what the Irish people are great at: we meet a person on holidays and within a day or two ye are the best of friends.

*

Partners often go away on holidays together early in their relationship. By then they've been going out together for a year, and it's time to ditch the mad holidays in the sun with the group of lads or lasses and to head off together so they can enjoy time with each other. Well, I'll never forget the first holiday I went on with Emma, now my wife. I had the disaster of all disasters, and to this day I have no idea how she's still with me. You'll enjoy this one . . .

Rory's Story: All Aboard

Back in 2006 myself and Emma went on our first holiday together, to Greece. I was nineteen, she was eighteen. Naturally enough, to prevent any awkwardness we drank a *lot*. One morning we woke up dreadfully hungover. Brains here had an idea and says, "Mon we go rent a speedboat for an hour. It'll clear the heads.' Even though Emma would rather have eaten sand than get on a boat while nursing a woeful hangover, she, as any young lassie would, said okay.

So off we headed in the speedboat. It was a seriously hot day, high 30s. Everything was going well – even fairly romantic, I'd say – when, all of a sudden, *bang!* Sure didn't the shagging engine go on us, and us in the middle of the ocean a fair bit out from shore. Disaster!

We panicked for a few minutes, as no-one was in an arse's roar of us. And didn't I get an unmerciful pain in my stomach. Now, I don't know about yous, but after a heavy night on the soup, the next day my bowels – well, let's just say they wouldn't be too reliable. *I don't believe this is happening. I badly need a shite*, I says to myself.

Emma looks at me and says, 'Eh, are you okay?'

I paused for a moment while hoping that this outrageous pain would go away. Then I just gave in. 'Jaysus, Emma, I'm so sorry, but I have to take a shite.'

'*What!*' says she.

'No, seriously, Emma. You can break up with me here and now if you need to, but I have to take a shite.' In that same moment sure didn't I leap overboard into the sea and let loose. Now, because I didn't pay much attention during physics classes – or at school in general, for that matter – I was under the impression that my waste would head straight to the bottom of the ocean. But, no, I suddenly found myself surrounded by my own disaster!

And it gets worse . . .

Just as I was looking up at Emma, ashamed as ashamed could be, didn't a Jaysus big huar of a boat come towards us, full of poxy tourists out spotting stupid dolphins.

'Aw, you're fuckin' *jokin'* me! Bollox. Look, Emma!' As she looked I ducked the head under the water till they passed, leaving poor Emma out in the open!

Afterwards I got back into the boat and tried to convince Emma that I wasn't a lunatic, claiming that I didn't know what had happened, and so on. Eventually a boat came out and guided us back to shore. Our evening meal was awkward enough that day!

Now there's a couple of things you should learn from this story. *Never* trust a speedboat engine. *Never* lamp a monster fry down on top of a feed of beer the night before. If you do, be sure to stay within a short distance from da jax the next day. And, finally, no matter how much of a disaster you think you are, there's hope for all of us.

St Patrick's Day

The most Irish day of the year. For some reason everyone around the world wants to be Irish for a day, because they presume that we do nothing all day but drink, tell stories and have the craic. To be fair, they aren't a million miles off!

I was born on St Patrick's Day, believe it or not, so I couldn't be any more Irish if I tried. I blame the famous day for my being fond of a few pints, because my birthday and the biggest piss-up of the year were always rolled up into one.

Rory's Story: A Saintly Birthday

One Paddy's Day, when I was only about fifteen, myself and a few of my buddies got the bus into town for the day. We had made a bombshell of mixed spirits from my 'drinks press' at home in the kitchen, and off we headed on the bus, slugging out of it in turns.

Town was crazy busy as always, all sorts of wannabe Irish people running about the place dressed like eejits. We chanced a couple of pubs until we got served. I was always huge for my age, so I already looked eighteen.

We started drinking in one pub and got chatting to these two American lasses. They were easily in their early twenties, but myself and my buddy chanced our arms in chatting them up.

'Yeah, we're in our second year of college here in Dublin. We play professional rugby, so we're on a scholarship with them. We play for the Irish team as well!'

'Oh, really? That's awesome!' Their eyes lit up. Jackpot, we thought to ourselves! So after a bit more of telling them what they wanted to hear, it wasn't too long before we were kissing them outside in front of the pub. I remember being well on at this stage, and the sun was beaming down, when all of a sudden I got a tap on the shoulder. 'Rory!' Who was it only my nosey auntie Sheila – what were the chances of that?

'Eh, Jaysus. Howaya, Sheila?'

'What are you doing here?'

Well, clearly I'm after striking gold with this lovely lass who thinks I'm twenty years of age, and you're doing me no favours! 'Ah, I'm just giving these two ladies directions to O'Connell Street.'

The two Philadelphia ladies weren't long in grabbing their handbags and heading in the other direction!

I spoke to my auntie for a minute – waffled the ears off her, no doubt – and off she went into the crowd. We staggered into two more pubs before running for the eight o'clock bus home.

The bus was packed. I was down the back of it as my mouth began to water and the bus begun to spin. Oh, no, I thought to myself, not the spins! So I battled and battled for about ten minutes until I couldn't battle any more. The mouth opened up and, like a fire hose, out came every last drop of beer, wine, vodka, whiskey, 7 Up, rum, Coke, burgers and chips, all over the bus. I had my buddy clapping me on the back to help me get it all up!

When I raised my bloodshot eyes the first person I saw was a woman who was on the local town committee with my mother. I still remember the look of disgust she gave me. Well, between my auntie and this auld biddy on the bus, my mother was finding out about my antics one way or another!

That day set the trend for Paddy's Days to come, but thankfully I'm a bit older and somewhat wiser now, so those messy Paddy's Days are all in the past. Well, kind of!

The St Patrick's Day parade

The Paddy's Day parade has become a massive event all over the world. If you come visiting Ireland for Paddy's Day you may not know that there's a huge difference between a city parade and a country one. At the city parade you'll be amazed at what kind of floats you'll see. A fair few bob and a lot of creativity has gone into giving these floats the X factor. You're likely to see state-of-the-art performers dressed up to the nines, dancing in sync and dazzling the crowds. You'll likely see a travelling circus with everything you can imagine!

On the other hand, if you really want a sense of Irish culture, tip along to a village parade. I remember being in my own local parade in Ashbourne when I was a young lad. For some reason it nearly always lashed rain on Paddy's Day, yet all of us under-10 footballers would be standing behind our club flag in our shorts and socks getting soaked to the bone!

Some of the floats you see at the small parades are priceless. You have an old 1977 banger of a car painted with Tricolours and two mad eejits pushing it down the road. The men have fags in the gob while they're waving at the crowd. You'll also see some sort of a tractor and trailer, and standing in the middle of it a nominated cow, wondering what she's done to deserve this! You might also witness the local celebrity dressed up as St Patrick at the helm of the parade.

When you think of St Patrick's Day you think of three things: Ireland, the colour green and alcohol. I can't see that changing any time soon!

Location, Location, Location: Irish-style

Growing Up in the Countryside v. in a Housing Estate

Whether you grew up in the sticks or in the city, there was fun to be had, but there was a massive difference between growing up in the countryside and growing up in a housing estate. I'm lucky enough to have witnessed how both camps operate. I grew up in a housing estate myself, and my cousins grew up in the countryside, so I had front-row seats to witness how different they are.

These are some features of growing up in a housing estate:

- It was all go – constant noise, cars moving, children playing.

- It was handy for knocking on your friends' doors. You knocked for them one after another until someone would finally come out to play.

- Sundays were not good, as most of the kids were away visiting relations.

- 🍀 There were games out on the road, including kerbs, tip the can, squares, three-in-one, volleys and red rover.

- 🍀 You had water fights on the road during the summer.

And this is the kind of thing you can expect growing up in the countryside:

- 🍀 You had a fifteen-minute bike journey to your nearest friend, but this was always a great adventure, with plenty of craic along the way.

- 🍀 You had endless banter on the farm, messing on the hay bales and driving tractors, from a young age.

- 🍀 It was easy to pretend to be Robin Hood or Rambo as you made weapons out of branches and went round the fields on a hunt. You weren't sure what you were hunting for, but your imagination took it from there.

It was an adventure when you got the go-ahead for going to the shop. You and your buddies were up on your bikes, and off you'd go. 'I'll be home when I'm home, Mammy.'

Growing Up on a Farm

When you're born on a farm you have very little choice but to learn the ropes from a very early age. You'll be assisting your parents about the place, whether it's helping in the fields and getting cow shite on your wellies for the first time, putting nuts in for the calves to eat or guarding gates so the cattle can't get into certain fields.

Now, a job you've been waiting a few years for is minding the gate so the cattle don't get into your neighbour's land. You feel important when you first hear those words. 'Rory, go stand beside Mooney's gate there and wave your stick as the cattle come by. Whatever you do, don't let them past you. Keep them on the road.'

You sprint over to your chosen position like a solider ready for action. You're nervous, of course, but excited all the same. As the cattle go by the gate thirty yards from you, it's show time. You hear the sound of them coming round the bend like a stampede, and you tense the body. The leader of the pack makes eye contact with you, and you send a message back through your eyes. 'Not today, pal. Not today.' You feel like Rambo but look like Stuart Little.

When most of them have been driven past the gate you get a bit cocky and give one of them a slap of the stick on the arse. 'Yuppp with ya!' you shout when you realise that you've completed one of your first jobs as a farmer. You walk proudly behind the cattle, and your father links up with you and gives you a real man's clap on the back. 'Well done, son.' You feel ten feet tall as you walk beside him. As far as you're concerned you already own ten acres, two hundred cattle and four tractors. Mission accomplished.

The Bog

Some people claim that you aren't even Irish unless you've served a day's work on the dreaded bog. The bog is where you find your true character. You're dropped there as young as six and told to stack turf until the sun goes down. I grew up as a 'townie', so I'd see the bog only once a year when I'd visit my cousins down in Co. Offaly – and once a year was plenty. When you're a soft housing-estate chap and you're landed on the bog to work for the day, you're like a fish out of water! Half an hour in and you're already bored, and your hands are in bits. Respect to all the young lads who spend most their summers on the bog: you boys have definitely earned your bacon and cabbage and have a solid reason to miss the odd training session!

Here's the survival kit you'll need to make sure you come through a day on the bog unharmed (if such a thing is possible!):

- Gallons of water
- Gallons of water
- Sun cream
- A terrible homemade ham sandwich
- Gallons of water
- Gallons of water.

People You Find in Every Irish Town and Village

The guard

The Garda Síochána, as you know, get plenty of slagging in this country. It's just in our genes to sneer at them. Ireland has to be the only country in the world where they're not really taken seriously.

Everyone has a guard as a friend, and it's a mystery to you how some of them are guards! There are three types of guard you'll come across in Ireland.

The **laid-back, sound guard** is the man you want to be meeting at a checkpoint. He joined up to earn a living and get a nice pension – full stop. He'll do his job but won't go out of his way to piss the public off. He'll always give ya the benefit of the doubt at a checkpoint.

You: Ah, bollox, a checkpoint.

Guard: Well, sir, do you know that your tax is out of date since last week?

You: I do, guard, I'm very sorry about that. It's in the post, and I should have it any day now. (You know well you never even applied for it!)

Guard: Okay. Sure listen: I'll let you off this time, but just make sure to pop it into that car as soon as it arrives. That fair enough?

You: That's bang on! Have a good day!

And he slaps the car and lets ya off! Phew! As you pull off, your back drowned in sweat, you feel blessed that you met a sound guard.

He'll do his shift and go home. A real decent skin!

The **geek of a guard**, however, is not the ideal fella to run into. He can be a sound man and is not an arsehole, really; he just takes his job far too seriously and does everything he was told to do below in Templemore during his training days. He'll let ya away with *nauthing!* One day over on your tax and it's out of the car you get! Everything he does is by the book. No amount of sweet talk will get you off the hook with this fella.

You: Ah, come on. I was only in the shop for one minute.

Guard: Sorry, but you're parking in a non-parking zone, which is against the law. I'm going to have to write you a ticket.

You: Ah, honest to God, I was only there for a minute. No need for a ticket!

Guard: I have to do my job, and do it right I will. Licence, please!

You: Fuck sake!

These fellas mean well, and I know they're just going by the book. But c'mon, lads. Lighten up a little!
The **complete bollox of a guard** is the one you really want to avoid! This fella doesn't suffer fools

gladly. If this guy gets up on the wrong side of the bed – which he does most mornings – you'll know all about it! This is the type of guard who'll walk the streets at 12:30 a.m. every Saturday, gawking into the windows of the local pubs to make sure serving has stopped.

You give this man any cheek whatsoever at a checkpoint and you'll be out of the car just as quick! He'll make you feel guilty even if you're as clean as a whistle. If he's in the station and you call in to report something, you'll have your work cut out for you!

You'll know the head on this fella a mile away as he come towards you on the street. There's a solid chance he was bullied at school and wants to be the bully of the bigger playground now. My advice when you come across this fella is to reply, Yes, sir, No, sir, Three bags full. You're better off in the long run!

The local biddy

If every village and town has a pub and a church, well, they'll also have this ear-to-the-ground lady. She's simply a walking gossip machine! She's the type of woman who knows more about you than you know about yourself. When you see her walking towards you it's head down or pretend you're on the phone. If you're unlucky enough to make eye contact and get stopped you'll be bombarded with the following questions:

- 🍀 How's your mother keeping? Is her foot any better after her fall? I'd get on to the council if I were her. That path she fell on was in a bad state. She might have a case there!

- 🍀 How's your father keeping? Is he still working?

- 🍀 How's college going? You're studying marketing, aren't you? What's that like? Are you commuting or staying below in Galway?

- 🍀 You look like you've lost weight, is that right?

- 🍀 Are you still going out with that lovely lady? What was her name again? She's from Tullamore, isn't she? I know her mother.

- 🍀 Do you still work part time in Tesco? I haven't seen you there in a while. Mind you, I haven't been in there lately. I prefer Aldi these days!

All these questions will be thrown at you before you've had a chance to take the earphones out. She'll more than likely stop two or three more people to hear their gossip while she has you pinned against the wall.

'Sorry, Rory. Ah, hello, Margaret, how are you keeping? Is John still on his tablets? I seen him yesterday, and he looks dreadful. My regards to him!'

Margret will walk on, and the auld biddy will turn back to you and tell you every last detail of Margaret's and John's business. Oh, these ladies are everywhere! My tip is to keep the eyes on the path at all times, because once they stop you it's very hard to get away without telling them what you've had for breakfast and what series you're watching on Netflix . . . You've been warned!

The local man hoping to become a TD

Everyone wants a seat in the Dáil these days – a handy number: talk some shite, earn a very tasty salary and a tidy little pension. There's guaranteed to be someone from your area who has become a TD or local politician at some stage. When the local elections are on you'll see his picture plastered over pillar and post.

Vote Number 1. Local man with local ideas to better OUR community.

What he really means is: Give me your vote, folks. Handy number it is. I'll promise ya whatever you want as long as you vote, but don't come annoying me with any problems once I'm elected!

Now, most of them are in it for the passion and will no doubt do a good job, but there's certainly one fella who might as well wear a cowboy hat and brandish a cap gun as he knocks on your door with a heap of leaflets. You hear him in the porch, and you try to hide, but often you've been caught and have to answer the door. When you do you're sure to find the following. He will

- be as well dressed as he has been since his wedding day and be clean shaven and have slick aftershave – the lot

- have a couple of his drinking buddies with him

- aim to come in for tea and tell you he's going to change the whole community for the better

- promise new playgrounds, a new GAA pitch, a games centre for teenagers and flowers planted throughout the village

🍀 show an interest in you and in your opinions about how to better your village or town.

Finally, after talking shite for twenty minutes, you'll make up some sort of a lie to try and get him out the door. 'I have to go and collect the kids, but thanks for calling.'

He'll leave by complimenting your tea-making skills, and off out the door he'll go to visit another house, drink more tea and promise the world to the next victim of bullshite o'clock!

One of two things will happen after this: he'll get elected, and twenty-seven years later a couple of flowers might appear beside the school playground; or he won't get elected, and he won't as much as smile at you on the street for the rest of time!

But, like I said, even though you'll no doubt occasionally get the genuine, passionate hard worker, you must also keep an eye out for the John Waynes of this business. They're everywhere come the local elections!

The GAA lotto man

This man appears in the corner of every pub on a Friday and Saturday night. You'll be having a few pints, and in pops Jimmy.

'Well, lads, GAA lotto. One for two euro or three for a fiver.'

'Good man, Jimmy. What's the jackpot?'

'Ten thousand euro. Yep, yep, ten thousand.'

'Really? Wow! When was it last won? It seems to be on that figure for as long as I can remember!'

'God, eh, good question. As far as I know, it was last won in August 1984.'

'1984, Jaysus, I wasn't even born then. That's a long time now without a winner. You're selling the tickets round the village for years, aren't ya, Jimmy?'

'I am. I started going round the pubs in September 1984.'

'Hah! That makes sense, Jimmy. Well, fair play to ya. Give me three for a fiver, there!'

'Thanks, men. The draw will take place up in Dinny's, Sunday night at nine o'clock. Good luck.'

How many GAA club lottos round the country haven't been won in years? Ah, well, your few bob is going towards a good cause either way, and without these great volunteers the GAA wouldn't be what it is.

The Irish farmer

One of the biggest characters in Irish society is the farmer. These men are the heartbeat of the countryside. Some say that farmers don't even bother having a passport. As any farmer's wife will tell you, it's hard enough to get them out of their county, never mind the country.

It's very easy to spot a farmer coming into his village or town. He'll be wearing

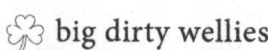

- 🍀 big dirty wellies
- 🍀 a farmer's cap
- 🍀 a pair of baggy, dusty trousers
- 🍀 a wild-looking shirt
- 🍀 an anorak swinging in the wind as he walks.

He might also be carrying a stick, without even noticing he has it on him!

The Local Facebook Group

As you know, Facebook is a very powerful tool in today's world. It can be great for keeping in contact with friends and family all over the world, and you can also wish people you barely know a happy birthday! But every town and village has the local Facebook noticeboard. These ladies and gents don't need to have a chat or a natter outside the local primary school any more: they can do it all on the internet. These are some of the topics brought up in these Facebook groups.

*

Hi, just to let you know, I spotted a red van driving around Summerville Avenue just now. The driver looks very suspicious. Spread the word!

Now, more than likely this fella got lost and passed by this person's house only twice, but those folk who have far too much time on their hands, and who spend most of that time gawking out the window, will smell trouble and be logged in to Facebook within seconds, warning the world of this dangerous man who's probably just looking for a house to price the laying of a few floors!

*

Hi, please see this rug, it's nearly brand new, but I'm offering it to the first person who DMs me. No charge, just need to collect it from my house. Thanks.

What they really mean is that they have no room to put this dusty, heavy, rotten-looking, 25-year-old rug in their garage, and it's too big for the black bin, so please come and take it off me as soon as you can!

*

Does anybody know what time Remo's takeaway opens? Thanks.

Most people will simply post the time it opens, but what they really feel like writing is: 'It's less hassle typing "Remo's takeaway opening hours" into a search engine, like a normal person, than it is asking three thousand people who are laughing at you!'

*

Hi, just to let you know, at 3 p.m. yesterday my son was walking home from school, and he said a man was looking at him. This man was cutting the grass in a high-vis jacket. He smiled and waved at my son. I'm very worried. Please let all parents be aware of this. This man could be very dangerous!

In reality a tidy-towns volunteer was cutting the grass and made eye contact with the boy and waved, like a normal person would. But now he has allegations made against him on Facebook by one of the noticeboard warriors! As the old saying goes, never believe anything you read on the internet, and local Facebook noticeboards are a prime example of that. Pinch of salt!

The Irish Pub

It may be that it has always been part of the culture, but Irish people spend a lot of time in the pub. We just love the craic, and nearly every event ends or begins in the pub.

- Weddings
- Funerals
- Birthdays
- Christenings, Communions, Confirmations
- Winning a match
- Losing a match
- Going through a bad time

☘ Going through a good time

☘ Looking for a bit of scandal and craic.

You might see certain people only in the pub. You won't see these people anywhere else! All types of people can be found in an Irish pub.

That creepy barman who tells the cringey jokes

This is the fella who tries to be cool all the time. He'll be landing one-liners on you all night. He'll often work in a hotel bar, and when you're having a quiet drink he'll be fully prepared with shite talk. This man will

☘ have greasy hair

☘ be banging of aftershave

🍀 have a pierced ear

🍀 wear a tight shirt

🍀 have fake teeth.

The genius of a barman

This man, gifted at his job, doesn't feel pressure. The bar could be wedged, but he'll always keep it cool. All it takes is for you to nod to him, and he'll have your round over to you before you're back from the jacks. He can poor a pint of stout, open a bottle of wine and cut a lime for your beer all in one go. He's a solid man to throw you a pint after hours; he's well tuned in and just naturally gifted! If only this man worked in every pub!

The auld owner

This man owns the place but does very little. He's a cute auld fox: he'll pop in to the pub, walk round chatting to a few familiar faces and throw the odd bit of turf on the fire in the bar as he stands there warming his arse. He'll have a shirt and tie on him at all times – a real old-school pub owner. Zero fear of him throwing you a free pint!

The nightclub bouncer

This man is hard to like. A lot of bouncers seem to have a chip on their shoulder. This is a standard conversation you'll have with these fellas:

'How's it going?'

'All right, lads. Where have ye been?'

'Ah, just had a couple of drinks at home.'

'You look like ye've had too much. Can't let ye in.'

'But sure we've only had a couple of bottles.'

'Sorry, lads, not tonight,' he says as he looks away and nods the head at a group of women and waves them in without question, even though one of them is leaning on her mate to stay steady! These fellas will

☘ have a shaved head

☘ be fond of the bench press – beach muscles!

🍀 have tattoos and earrings

🍀 think they're Rambo.

Of course, they're not all like this, and you do get some sound ones, but for every sound one you'll have to put up with three arseholes!

The bar-stool bullshitter

This fella will be at the bar waiting on another poor unfortunate ear to burn and talk shite to. He's that much of a waffler that he's come to believe his own lies! Apparently, this fella

🍀 has played for Man United

🍀 has won an all-Ireland with Dublin

🍀 owns three different companies

🍀 drives a Range Rover

🍀 has to strap his 'manhood' to his knee

🍀 has visited thirty-five countries

🍀 has competed in the Olympics

🍀 owns a helicopter

🍀 has a model girlfriend

🍀 has achieved all this by sitting at the bar sipping pints. Imagine that!

Once you make eye contact with this fella you head in the other direction, or if you're out in the smoking area, and he wanders out, the fag won't be long put out, and back inside with you as fast as you can!

The oddball

Every pub has this man sitting in the corner. Not too many know his name or dare to ask him. He just sits there sipping on the one pint all day, sussing everyone out. He won't be caught smiling, nor having the craic. He almost looks like a spy, in there investigating everyone. You speak to him only when he speaks to you. When he does speak it will be very few words. Not making any attempt at eye contact he'll say, 'Not great weather out there.'

'It's not, no. A lot warmer in here, anyway. Did you see the match earlier?'

He'll then give you a stern look but make no reply, not because the score had any effect on him but because he has no interest in any more talking. He's said his part to you, and that's it. This is when you walk away, for your own safety. These bucks are generally harmless, but I wouldn't fancy confirming that idea!

The non-drinker

Yes, believe it or not, these do exist in Ireland. When you're in the pub and they're asked what they want to drink, and they say 7 Up, you reply, 'Ah, are you on antibiotics?'

This causes them to utter the astonishing words 'No, I don't actually drink, to be honest.'

This is when the whole pub takes a deep breath, before saying, *'You don't drink!'*

In most countries it's considered quite normal not to drink, but in Ireland you'll get a quare look. Sure why would you not drink, people say. But if you don't drink

- you're fresh all the time and have no regrets, and you don't have to experience the dreaded *beer fear*

- you have more money in your pocket

- you can drive anywhere you like after a visit to the pub.

But in Ireland all this doesn't appeal to that many people. We'd gladly avoid all the freshness, and we have no regrets about that one mental weekend when the craic was ninety and when we made enough memories to last a lifetime!

Popular drinks

Irish people love a few drinks, and here are the most popular drinks among us. Certain drinks, of course, suit certain scenarios.

A large bottle of **Bulmer's**. This cider is most popular during the summer days, out in the beer garden. Some fellas can drink these till the cows come home, and not a bother on them! The pear-flavoured one made an appearance a couple of years ago but didn't last too long on the market. (It lasted about as long on the market as it did in your stomach! I'll say no more.) But a large bottle of the apple cider, with loads of ice, is a summer favourite for many.

Dutch Gold, Devil's Bit, Linden Village. The taste of your teenage years, these were the most popular drinks when you had no money and shouldn't have been drinking. How many of you got six cans of a Friday night but actually drank all six? There isn't one person who isn't guilty of having pulled the old 'I'm going for a piss' and bringing their can with them to pour some of it down the toilet! If you say you haven't done this at least once during your teenage years, you're lying!

I don't know which tastes worse, the end of a can of Dutch Gold or the dregs of two litres of Linden Village from a bottle that's been being lying around on a warm summer's evening. But sure who was giving out when you were sixteen in a field having the craic with your friends!

Gin and tonic. This, let's be honest, is not a cheap drink, but it has been getting more and more popular over time. The gin and tonic in the big fishbowl glass – a solid choice for the hard-working ladies in the office of a Friday night or for the fella who can't stomach any more pints! Either way, this combo has made its way up the chart of Ireland's favourite drinks. If you're a G & T fan, you might get yourself signed up to one of those gin cruises – a bit of paradise for all you gin heads out there!

Whiskey. The choice of many a raw man, including my father. 'Jameson with a drop of water.' It's a drink people turn to during good times and bad; how good and how bad determines the amount of whiskey that's dropped into the glass. This drink makes most of its appearances at house parties during singalongs. When there's nothing else left to drink in the house you turn to the whiskey. When Tommy is in the middle of forgetting the words to 'The Green Fields of France' he'll have a glass poured for him in a dirty cup taken from the dishwasher!

Jägerbombs. Ah, the good auld Jägerbombs. Where would you be without them on a night out these days? It's the definition of a 'pick me up' drink. There's always one person on a night out in every gang who's a huar for these. You'd have only three pints sunk, and down this fella arrives with a round of Jägers. Straight away you know that a 'few quiet pints' has now, with just the one Jägerbomb, turned into a rip-roaring session! That's how powerful these lads are – rocket fuel!

A pint of **Guinness**. By a country mile, this is the drink most associated with Ireland. Now, there's a bit of passion involved in this statement: nothing, and I mean *nothing*, compares to a great pint of porter.

Only Guinness-drinkers will understand me when I say that the difference between a good pint of stout and a bad one is just incredible! You can have a bad pint of lager and get away with it, but 'Arthur's soup' is miles apart. What's amazing about Guinness is that the fancier the place is, the more likely it is that the pint will be shite. But if you go into a kip of a place where the pint is cheap, the chances are you'll get a pint of mother's milk. This is all about the pour and where the keg is stored, so they say. They reckon the closer the keg is to the tap, the better the pint will be, which is why you rarely get a good pint of plain in a hotel, where the kegs are usually a treasure hunt away from the taps.

After you finish a pint of porter you'll know it was a good one if you can see the rings of each sup in your glass. Then you're onto a winner. If your glass is clear and nearly ready to put back up on the shelf, well, then you know you've just had a crap pint. It's as simple as that!

Guinness brought out these new pint glasses a couple of years ago, but the Guinness lovers, including myself, were not too happy about it. It just doesn't taste the same, for some reason. You know an experienced Guinness drinker when they ask, 'Can I have my pint in the old pint glass, please?' So if anyone high up in Guinness somehow happens to read this book, take note: your customers want the old glasses back. As the old saying goes, 'If it's not broken, don't fix it.'

Still, drinking a pint of Guinness on a cold December evening, in front of a fire, with a couple of bags of Bacon Bites and sound company – that's up there with life's great pleasures. I'll drink to that!

Hangovers

It would be foolish of me to write about drinking and not go in depth into the pain that alcohol can bring to you mentally and physically. When the drinking and craic have stopped, your body has to endure the dreaded hangover. Oh, God, is there anything worse than a dirty hangover? What's frightening about them is that they worsen the older you get!

To break it down for you, this is how a typical hangover usually goes. You wake up, blinking your eyes as you try to make sense of where you are and what's going on. You soon figure out that you're in your own room (thank fuck!). You move your tongue round in your mouth, but it's difficult to do so, because your gob is as dry as the back of a flip-flop! The sharp, thumping pain kicks in now, and the realisation has hit you. 'Aw, no! The hassle of this. Ugh! Dying!'

Before you pull yourself out of bed you grab your phone off the bedside locker and bravely check your social media. Snapchat is not a good place to start: you'll see all the scutter you were up to on your story. The *fear* starts from there.

You put down the phone, as you can't deal with looking at any more of your carry-on from the night before. You pull your jeans up off the floor, reefing out your wallet, only to find nothing in it but a heap of change. There's not one note to be seen, only a laser-card receipt for six Jägerbombs at 1:19 a.m., in a nightclub you promised yourself the previous weekend you'd never step foot in again. 'You're a fucking eejit,' you say to yourself as you crumple up the receipt.

You ring a friend who was with you to see what he remembers of the night, but he's in bad shape as well, so you both decide that the best thing to do is to go for an auld breakfast roll.

It's about now that you get a fit of the giggles – one minute you're laughing away but you're pure raging with yourself the next. This happens all day long: great form, dreadful form. You lie low all day, waiting for the takeaway to open. The only thing that excites you now is the prospect of a big Chinese or pizza that evening.

You're very tempted to go for the 'cure': even two pints will make you feel better, you tell yourself. But, as we all know, them two pints can lead to another huar of a session in the blink of an eye! You stay strong, because you know it's only prolonging the *fear* if you go at it again!

It's finally evening time, so it's time to mill the takeaway. No matter what you select you always regret it, and you're bulling that you didn't go for something different. Again, that's the bad form playing tricks on you. You horse the food into ya and feel like complete and utter shite five minutes after you've given up trying to finish it. You then start munching on all sorts of crap in the house: crisps, cakes, bars – whatever is the most unhealthy you'll crave!

You flick through various programmes on Netflix, dreading that time when you have to hit the hay so you can be in some shape for work the next day. This is when you come face to face with the toughest part of your hangover: the night horrors!

You're almost frightened getting into bed. Even though you're wrecked tired, you know there's not much chance of you sleeping. Your heart rate is still trying to come back to normal after the vodka and Red Bull. You eventually fall asleep, but you soon wake up full sure that's it's nearly time for work, only to realise that you're only asleep twenty-nine minutes! 'Oh, no,' you think to yourself. You jump on your phone then for a while to flick though the same auld shite on Facebook, Instagram and Twitter.

You do this a few times before eventually falling back asleep. You fall into a deeper sleep this time, but you have a horrific dream in which the most dreadful things imaginable happen to you. Then, just as the nightmare hits its peak, you leap up from the mattress. 'Get out the fuck. I'll kill you!' You're convinced that there's someone in your room, and you feel the beads of cold sweat on your forearm. You tell yourself over and over again that it's just the drink, that everything will be grand. Your mind beats the shite out of you about money, about stuff you said to people the night before. Even the most stupid thing can be built up in your mind when you have the *fear*. The phrase 'I'm not drinking again' goes through your mind all night long.

'It's just not worth it. It fucking isn't. This is absolute torture!'

You finally fall into a lovely sleep about fifteen minutes before the alarm on your phone goes off, vibrating on the locker. And there you have it: Monday morning. You feel like shite, you have no money and now you have to face the real world. But after you get a bit of decent food into you and do some exercises, and then sleep better during the week, you're ready to do it all over again the following weekend. Such is life in the fast lane!

Living Abroad

Not many nations in the world are as well dispersed as the Irish. We're everywhere! No matter where you travel you'll run into an Irish person at some point. You get chatting to each other, and before you know it you've made a connection.

'Whereabouts are you from, yourself?'

'I'm from Co. Westmeath.'

'Really, what part?'

'Just outside Kinnegad.'

'Kinnegad! You hardly know the Dalys, do you?

'John and Lucy?'

'Yeah! They're my first cousins.'

'That's gas. I know them well. I used to hurl with John.'

'God, it's a small world, isn't it!'

Whenever the country hits a recession, plenty of young people pack up and head off to try and find a better quality of life. Australia has been a very popular destination for the Irish to head to. Sure why wouldn't they? Nice weather, good money to be earned and no auld biddy gossiping about their antics outside Mass of a Sunday morning! Here's exactly what happens to the Irish when they move 'down under'.

So you've had enough of this country and decide to head to Oz. You save up as much as you can, kiss Mammy goodbye and off you go. Some people who have never even left their village take their first trip outside the country to one of the countries furthest from Ireland! The trip is a killer. No matter what way you look at it, you're going to be on the plane for more than twenty hours.

The lucky ones can treat the flight as a sleeping marathon and lie back and relax all the way to

Australia, but a lot of people struggle to sleep on planes, and for them it can be a very long ordeal. They try to concentrate on watching films, despite their arse constantly going dead and the big eejit in front of them letting their seat back for the whole journey. And let's not even mention the food! You'll also probably have had a big shindig of a going-away party a couple of days before you left. So you're getting on the plane already banjoed!

When you eventually land in Australia you no longer know your arse from your elbow. You haven't got a clue what time or even day it is. You're just happy to be on solid ground.

Most emigrating Irish people have someone they know living abroad who they tend to hook up with while they're finding their feet. There's no better place to settle in and ease the homesickness than Bondi in Sydney. It's become that much of a home for the Irish in Sydney that it's been nicknamed 'County Bondi'. Most sensible people will actually advise you to avoid Bondi, because it's such a perfect place for getting into your comfort zone.

There's many an Irishman and Irishwoman who have planned to travel the world for a year or two, but once they land in Bondi Junction, because the craic there is so good, they don't see anywhere else.

You have the tea gardens and you had the famous Cock 'n' Bull pub (which I believe has sadly just closed, in 2018) – a mighty place in which to have the craic and feel like you're at home.

After arriving most people will suss out some sort of accommodation and say to themselves that they'll enjoy a week or so of fun and then start looking for work. But that week quickly turns into a month of madness, beaches, pints, sunburn, beach pints, sunburn, mid-week tea gardens and leaping round to the famous Bacon and Cabbage duo in the Bull of a Sunday as they belt out tunes by the Wolfe Tones. You might as well be at home in your local, given how little of Australia you'll have seen.

Before you know it the funds are low and it's time to start looking for work. For men, the most common place to head for is the building site. Good money and good craic, and you start early and finish early! There aren't many sites around the world that haven't got at least one Irishman on it. We're known as solid workers abroad, and that reputation has been in place for donkey's years. Sure we built half of America, didn't we!

One of the drawbacks of living abroad is that it can be tough to get the most-loved Irish products. Ya can forget about drinking Guinness, for starters.

There's an old saying that Guinness doesn't travel, and, my God, it is correct. Just ask for a pint of stout when you land in Australia and you'll know all about it! You'll often spot the bartender pulling the pint straight up. There's no such thing as letting it settle or topping it up: it's just poured like a pint of lager and handed to you.

So I'm afraid your days of drinking porter are over while you're down under. Well, unless you're a sow and would drink anything. In that case fire away, but don't say I didn't warn ya!

Good-quality chocolate and sausages are two more products that don't travel well. You'll crave an auld Denny's sausage the morning after a few pints, but decent sausages are very hard to come by in Australia. And let's not even mention the famous Irish teabags!

Because of this you'll often put in a request to home. The emergency package delivered from your beloved mother needs to contain the following:

- **Crisps.** Mighty Munch, Chipsticks, Meanies, Hula Hoops, Tayto salt and vinegar.

- **Chocolate.** Has to be all Cadbury's: Moros, Whispas, Dairy Milks, Double Deckers, etc.

🍀 **Teabags.** Barry's or Lyons, depending on your preference. Cheap ones from Aldi or Lidl are not acceptable.

🍀 Curry sauce, gravy, jelly and so on.

To request your package you may have to endure the dreaded Skype call to the parents. Now, of course you miss your parents when you're living abroad, and you like catching up with them for the gossip back home. But a Skype call to Irish parents can be an ordeal, as the time difference is tough to manage!

It's always a Monday evening for you, so you're fairly shattered after the weekend. But you've put Mammy off for three weeks now, so you have to get it done. You get the phone or laptop and head off into your room. Parents mean well, but they ask the same questions every time you speak to them from abroad.

🍀 What time is it there now?

🍀 Have you much work on?

🍀 I hope you're saving your money and not drinking it all.

🍀 Is it hot there? God, I wouldn't be able for that weather.

🍀 Did you run into anyone you know?

🍀 Not much news here. Your father says hello.

🍀 Have you any plans to come home?

🍀 Ah, this country is a joke. My pension is being cut again.

🍀 The lads won on Sunday.

🍀 What's wrong with you? You're in dreadful form.

You try to let them go about ten times before they actually hang up. 'Right, I'll let you go, Mam. The internet is acting up here! I'll be chatting to you soon. Love you. Good luck!' That's that out of the way for another couple of weeks, says you!

*

I lived in Australia for a year myself back in 2010, and I'll tell ya a story that sums up us Irish down under!

Rory's Story: Home and Away in Australia

A few years ago, like most Irish people nowadays, myself and the missus headed off to Australia to see what all the fuss was about. We settled in Sydney and travelled round from there.

One day we were both off work and said we'd do something together. Now, as would be the case for most Irish lads, a day out sightseeing doesn't appeal to me in the slightest. It bores the hole off me, to be honest! We had a row over a few ideas before picking a winner. Both of us are huge 'Home and Away' fans, so we said we'd head to Palm Beach (Summer Bay in the series) for a nice day trip. We hopped on the bus and headed down. Emma, being an organised woman, packed us a few things. I, on the other hand, big lug that I am, brought my wallet, a Meath jersey (typical gobshite wanting to tell the world I'm Irish), a pair of shorts and a hat to prevent my baldy head from getting scalded.

We touched down after an hour or so of travelling. We were having a great day. Jaysus, it's a grand spot, I must say. We said we'd go for a walk along the beach before we got a bit of grub. It was a nice sunny day, not much of a breeze – perfect stuff. We strolled along the shore as the water lapped round our feet. Very relaxing altogether! Then, out of nowhere, didn't a huar of a wave catch me off balance. Being the awkward ogre that I am, I wobbled and eventually landed on my arse, absolutely soaked with a mouthful of pissy, salty water . . . *Lovely*.

I eventually dried off and, with the crack of my arse smothered in sand, we said we'd get the spuds.

The food was class. I went for the casual lunch: BLT and chips. You can't bate it. As I went to pay I reached into the pocket, and there was *nothing* to be found. The alarm bells began sounding!

'Emma, eh, do you have the wallet?' I says to her in an awful worried tone. I knew well I'd left the house with it!

'No, sure you had it!' and just like that we made eye contact and both thought, Ahh, ballix!

The fucking salty water must have gobbled up my purse, which contained a couple of hundred dollars, my safe pass for the sites and my monthly bus pass. *Nightmare!*

Now, bullshitting the waitress, telling her we were 'just popping out to the ATM to get cash' and would be back in a minute, was handy enough. (I'm not proud of it, but sure what else could I say!) The big problem was that we only had one hape of dirt of a phone with us, which, typically, had just run out of credit! How the feck were we going to get home!

I was just going to have to explain what had happened to the bus-driver and hope he was a decent skin and would let us on. This would be like a man from India stepping on a Bus Éireann coach in Mullingar and trying to get a free journey to Termonfeckin. My work was cut out for me.

We were sitting at the stop for ages, the sun beaming down on us, waiting for a poxy bus to arrive. Both of us, as you can imagine, were getting very, very pissed off with the situation, and of course I was getting constantly bollocked out of it by the missus for losing the wallet, as if I took the shaggin' thing out of my pocket and threw it into the ocean for the pure craic.

'*Jesus Christ*, woman, it was a fucking accident, and if you keep at it I'll speak only for myself when this bus arrives, and you can make your own way home!' Her giving out soon calmed down.

Now picture this: I stepped up onto the packed bus that eventually arrived togged out in a Meath jersey, and I had a pair of horrible auld Penney's shorts and a dorky Titleist hat, which I'd robbed before I'd left Ireland, on the auld head. If that wasn't enough, I had on the cheapest, most worn-down pair of flip-flops you can imagine. They were size 12, and I'm size 14, so my big toes were sticking out over the edge. I looked a right state.

I just took one deep breath and said, 'Well, how's things? Listen, I'm from Ireland, and I came down here because I'm a huge fan of "Home and Away", so I wanted to have a look at Summer Bay. We ended up going for a walk along the beach, and didn't a wave hit me – knocked me over and robbed my wallet! Can myself and my girlfriend please get on for free?'

I stood there with a pure browned-off head on me, not knowing what he was going to say or do. He looked me up and down and began to laugh his head off, saying in a fine Cork accent, 'Hah! Not a bother, *booiiieee*. Hop on, there!'

The Irish in the Middle East

A lot of Irish people now live in the Middle East, especially in places like Dubai, Abu Dhabi and Qatar. These places have become especially popular for primary school teachers, because of better pay, no taxes and the chance to experience a very difference culture. I've visited those three places myself in the past number of months, doing a few gigs and attending GAA functions. The GAA in these places is massive. It's a great springboard for people to meet each other, avoid homesickness and, most important, have a good social life!

You would think, it being the Middle East, that there wouldn't be too much drinking going on. It's frowned on in much of that part of the world, and it's not cheap for a pint. I ordered a pint with my dinner the first evening I was in Dubai, and it was the equivalent of about €12. I nearly had a heart attack when I worked it out! I wouldn't mind, but it was cat. The head was gone off it within a few minutes, but do you think there was any chance of me paying €12 for a pint but leaving it behind me? Not likely!

What they do have, though, is this thing called a 'brunch'. Now, this is not the brunch you're familiar with. This set-up in the Middle East is a piss-up of the highest order. For about €90 you can eat and drink as much as you want for five hours. Now, I'm not talking just beer, wine and cocktail sausages: this is an outrageous spread. If you want twenty Jägerbombs, that's no bother. If you want a steak, if you want gin and tonic – literally anything you want you can have, and it doesn't even end there. When those five hours of madness are over you can pay another €70 for a 'liquid brunch', which is just the drinks package, for another four hours. So, as anyone who has taken part in this Friday session will tell you, you're in a bundle come eight o'clock and fit for the bed.

What's even more worrying about this is that, if that kind of thing went on at home, you'd stumble out into the streets, singing and acting the eejit, and head straight to the chipper. But you can't do this in the Middle East! The minute you walk outside it's game-face time, because if you get into a taxi and start acting the bollox – sneering and jeering at the taxi man – them boys will bring you straight to the cop shop, and it's lights out: you'll be deported within days.

I did the double brunch in Dubai with a group of Irish people a couple of years ago, and, as you can imagine, the messing and craic does be unreal. Live bands on all day – the lot. When it hit eight bells I went up to my room to get changed, and I came back down to meet them again for more antics. I staggered into the toilet, and the next minute I woke up sitting on the jacks – but it was 4:37 a.m. 'Ah, Jaysus, me head.'

It's definitely worth experiencing if you're ever in the Middle East. You'll run into the Irish gang and will have some craic, but I wouldn't fancy doing it every weekend. The *fear* at home is tough to cope with, but out there it's a different ball game – not to mention the heat of forty degrees!

Favourite Irish Sports

Mad about Sports

Irish people love sports – we really do! Nothing sums us up better than a soccer tournament. The support is incredible! Even though we're always one of the outsiders in the very few tournaments we qualify for, it doesn't stop us heading to the venues in our thousands. The credit unions are hit hard, and we tell them everything they want to hear so that we can get the loan.

'Yeah, we've been waiting a long time to do up our kitchen. It's in bad need of a make-over, so we'd really appreciate the loan to help us make this happen.'

But what you're really thinking is: 'As you know, Ireland rarely qualify for a major tournament, and myself and all the lads, even though we're in our forties now, have been waiting for this day a long time. So please give me €8,000 so I can go and have, without doubt, the greatest two weeks of my life. That fair enough?'

Every man's suitcase heading to these tournaments will include the following:

🍀 2 Irish jerseys

🍀 10 pairs of boxers

🍀 3 tubs of Sudocrem

🍀 an Irish flag

🍀 T-shirts and shorts

🍀 fuck all else!

Before every match Ireland is involved in, your local town or village is a sea of green. Nobody brings the banter like the Irish people do, packing out all the bars, drinking cans on the streets, singing the ballads, getting the atmosphere going.

You'd often wonder – not that we care – what the other countries looking at us do be thinking. Sure Ireland could be four nil down at half time, yet the Irish fans will be in full flow, singing, 'It's so lonely round the fields of Athenry ... Lowwww lieeee ...'

'Wissen die Iren nicht dass sie vier-nil verlieren?' says the German gawking at us from the far stand of the stadium!

The GAA

Imagine writing a book about Ireland and not talking about the GAA! It would be like writing a book about New Zealand and not mentioning rugby! As many of you know, I'm a massive GAA man, and I covered every corner of the GAA world in my previous book, *The Rory's Stories Guide to the GAA.*

Lifelong friendships are often developed in the GAA, whether it's you starting off in your local club as a five-year-old acorn, spotting your old buddies from junior infants, or making a county panel and becoming the best of friends with a fella from a club you don't like! It has to be the most professional non-professional sport in the world, but I think that this is what makes it: folks giving their time for the love of the game. From the parents washing jerseys to the selectors on the under-12 hurling team, from the water boys all the way up to the county stars, it's all one big family!

Now, don't get me wrong: if local rivals meet each other in a big club championship match there isn't too much love lost there. In fact, many a couple have fallen out over their love for their respective clubs. There won't be too much spoken over dinner that night, I can assure you.

Nothing defines us mad Irish more than the GAA. No matter what town or village you pass through you'll find a GAA pitch. It's the heartland of every community. This is the grass roots of the GAA, as they call it, and a great number of people give up their time for the cause.

Your club will be filled with the many characters who shape the GAA. What's crazy is that every club in the country is exactly the same. You think your club is the only one with the grumpy groundsman who treats the pitch like his family; with the mother who loses the rag on the sideline; with the dodgy umpire; with the lunatic supporter; with the auld bollox who has nothing good to say; with the fella who's always injured; with the cocky nuisance who thinks he's *classss*.

Well, you're not alone. Every GAA club in the country has all these personalities in it, which is what makes the sport unique. You make so many friends through the GAA, and the GAA experience abroad sums this up. People who move abroad for work and who haven't played GAA since their glory under-14 days will often take up the sport overseas, because it's a great way to socialise and make friends. We Irish are very clannish when we move abroad, simply because we get each other's humour and ways. That's why the GAA abroad is such a massive help to everyone finding their feet. The GAA is one of the very few things to have benefited from the recession in the late 2000s, because it grew legs, and since then you'll do well not to find a GAA club in every part of the world. Magic!

Poor Mayo

On the inter-county front, no group of supporters sums up the obsession with the GAA quite like the poor Mayo fans. My God, how loyal they are to their team! Consider that they have witnessed their county lose no fewer than nine all-Ireland finals since they last tasted success in 1951. Yet they keep coming back, year after year, in their throngs to support the men in green and red. You have to visit such places as Westport, Belmullet and Ballyhaunis to really get a sense of how mad these people are for Mayo GAA.

I did a gig down in Ballyhaunis before the 2016 all-Ireland final, and after the show we went to a pub. A few pints were had while we were discussing, in depth, the coming final against the Dubs. Well, before I knew it it was 2 a.m. The doors were locked, the ashtrays were handed out and the craic was only getting started. What did they do only stick on a couple of old finals on the telly! The 1996 final (that massive row with Meath) and the 2013 final (against Dublin) they had on two different tellys, so you could watch whichever one you were in the humour for! I thought this was nuts: why would they want to watch these finals again and remind themselves of the misery? They must have watched these games a hundred and one times, but here they were sculling porter at 3:06 a.m., analysing the games to death.

'That's where we lost it, John.'

'Ah, God, if only he'd laid it off, that was game over.'

'That was such a costly mistake, wasn't it? Christ!'

I was looking round thinking how crazy this was but also how much I'd love to see this tribe of the most loyal of fans – not just in the GAA world but in all of sport – taste just one day in paradise. God knows they deserve it! Who knows, maybe 'Mayo for Sam' will be sung until that day finally arrives, and when it does I for one will be heading to Castlebar for the week. There won't be a session like it ever witnessed again!

Rugby: The Six Nations

The Six Nations is another tournament during which we all jump on the bandwagon and let on we're George Hook. It always happens between February and March, so I think the main reason we get so much behind it is that a lot of people would have done dry Januarys and are looking for any excuse for a few pints of a Saturday afternoon in February. This is a standard conversation about rugby between husband and wife:

'Where are you going dressed like that?'

'Like wha'!'

'In that new rugby jersey.'

'Sure Ireland are playing Italy in the first round of the Six Nations today. I'm heading down to Molloy's to watch it with few of the lads. It won't be easy: the Italians always have one good game in them.'

'Since when have you become such a rugby expert?'

'Ah, I love the rugby!'

'Ya mean ya love having an excuse for pints.'

'Ah, no, I'm really looking forward to this match. I'll see ya tonight.'

And off he heads down the road in his spanking new Ireland jersey.

He'll be the very man during the match.

'What's a bleedin' ruck?'

'What do ya mean, offside!'

'It's very scrappy, isn't it?'

'Size of some of them fellas – big apes!'

*

There's a glaring difference between rugby and other sports: the respect the crowd give the kicker. Have you ever been at a match, or even seen it on the telly, and witnessed the sheer respect the crowd gives the kicker? You'd hear a slurp from a straw when the kicker is about to take aim.

I was once at a Leinster match, and just as Johnny Sexton was getting ready to launch another one between the posts some fella up on the top stand roared, 'Hon, Johnny, ya boy, ya.' Well, my God, you should have seen the reaction from the crowd! The looks they all threw up towards him, the man might as well have committed manslaughter!

So a word of advice: if you ever attend an important rugby match and have a few pints on you, do refrain from shouting, talking or even whispering during the kicks for goal. Otherwise you could be escorted out and never be seen at a rugby match again! You have been warned!

Referees: The kings of rugby

No official elicits more respect and authority, in any sport, than the rugby referee. If the GAA or soccer ref makes a call during play he gets an absolute earful of abuse from the players.

'Are ya blind, ref?'

'Ref, you're useless!'

'Stick on a green jersey, ref.'

But in rugby he's the boss. Players are afraid of him, and rightly so. I do find it funny that all these absolute beasts of men, even in the heat of battle, still have the temper to respect to the ref. 'Sorry, ref, my apologies.' Some difference there: in a junior B club game between fierce rivals the refs are lucky to come off the pitch unharmed!

Golf

The game of golf is becoming more and more popular among the Irish. Granted, we have some of the nicest courses in the world, with our lovely scenery, but they have to be closed for a good part of the year because of grey skies and lashing rain.

The US Masters comes round once a year, and this is another prime example of the Irish people jumping on the bandwagon! You go to any driving range or open golf course during the Masters and the place will be busy with all types of fellas thinking they're Tiger Woods! They'll watch the Masters, think the game is easy and buy the best set of clubs and clothing, then land down to the first tee box and take three fresh airs before even connecting with the ball. You'll find some mad characters on a golf course, ranging from the inexperienced to yer man who thinks he's Rory McIlroy.

The fella who has the best of gear but is pure shite

This man will invest most of his salary in his clubs: state-of-the-art driver, massive bag. One of his golf balls will cost €10, and he'll have branded wet gear – the lot. His only problem is that he can't hit the ball out of his way!

The cheater

Any chance this fella gets he'll be acting the bollox. Somehow he always gets a lovely lie in the rough, and whenever his ball goes into the ditch he's always okay to look for it himself – and somehow he always finds it! Cowboys, Ted!

The fella who loses the head every second hole

You want to keep your distance from this lad on the golf course. He goes through more putters and drivers than a PGA professional. If you're in his company and he misses a three-foot putt you better hide behind your golf bag, because this man's putter is being slung over your head and into the nearest lake. He was a lunatic on the hurling field during his playing days, and he isn't much better on a golf course.

The auld lad who's just class

Ya can't bate experience, and this man has it flowing out of him. It's actually annoying how consistent he is. You could smash a driver a hundred yards past him every hole, but he's so steady he'll always grind you down! He won't have the best of clubs. In fact, he'll more than likely have a crap set and won't even wear a golf glove, but he's playing golf the last seventy years and knows every bump and roll on the course. Class is permanent!

The fella obsessed with the rules

This is without doubt the worst guy to play golf with. A nerd of the highest calibre, he'll be more concerned about what you're doing during your round than about playing himself. A natural dork during his schooldays, he has carried this into his adult life, and he lets it out on the golf course.

'Sorry, it's a one-shot penalty if you ground your club in a bunker. Just letting you know!'

'Sorry, Einstein. I'll make sure not to upset you!'

This player's name is one you'll be avoiding on the time sheet when you're looking for a game on Saturday afternoon down the local!

The Irish Language

Níl a Fhios Agam

In all honesty, there aren't many countries that have a native language that half the population are barely able to string a sentence together in. I'm embarrassed to say that I'm one of these people: I remember only one or two sentences in Irish from my schooldays.

If I travelled to parts of Co. Kerry or Co. Donegal where it's full-on Irish-speaking the local people would leave me out in the garden with the dog at night. I just couldn't get the hang of the language in school. Part of it was not listening to teachers, of course, but it would just not register with me. The relationship between spelling and pronunciation is quite different from English. People with Irish names living abroad must have a hard time, as we know from Saoirse Ronan explaining in every American interview how her first name is pronounced. If you were to say these names to anyone outside Ireland, this would be their attempt at spelling them:

- Aoife: *Eefa*
- Sadhbh: *Sive*
- Bláthnaid: *Blawnid*

🍀 Caoimhe: *Qweeva*

🍀 Saoirse: *Seersha*.

When you're abroad and meet, say, Dutch or Belgian people in a random bar, they'll apologise for their poor English, even though it's perfect and probably their third language! So then you have to pretend that you're fluent in Irish too: you don't want to let the auld country down. 'Yeah, we actually have our own *native* language.' Then the shite hits the fan when they ask you to say something in it. You'd always go for the baker one, 'Is maith liom cáca milis,' because that's one of the few lines that all children learn fairly quickly in school!

Having our own language is something to be very proud of, but unfortunately, as is the case for me and a good chunk of Irish people, many of us don't have too many words of it!

TG4

This famous Irish-speaking TV channel is loved by all. You never know what you'll find on TG4 – everything from the Tour de France to the mad soap 'Ros na Rún', our version of 'EastEnders' but with a quarter of the budget. You're guaranteed to come across a three-hour American western here and there. Auld lads love getting stuck in to them, but, personally, I'd rather watch my football shorts drying on the line!

It's a really impressive channel in its coverage of sports, especially GAA and rugby. There's nothing like flicking through the telly and randomly coming across a great GAA match from 'back in the day': lads beating the heads off each other and the ref waving play on. They also have a brilliant GAA programme, 'Laochra Gael', in which they do an interview with a GAA legend about their career – always a great watch.

The Gaeltacht

Another very Irish thing to do when you're growing up is to tip along to the Gaeltacht with a few of your school buddies. Parents of course want you to go and brush up on your Irish, but, even more than that, they want some peace and quiet for the few weeks you're gone.

For that brief time during the summer you're the problem of your bean an tí. It's a bit mad when you think about it, being sent to a different part of the country and staying in a stranger's house for a few weeks while your parents are at home enjoying the most of the freedom. It's the luck of the draw with mná tí as well. You could be stuck with a really strict one who feeds you rotten food and gives you the glare any time you utter a word of English, or you could be with a sound one who's well stocked in Wagon Wheels and turns a blind eye if you're trying to sneak out.

The thoughts of that number of Irish classes is terrifying to a teenager, but the fear disappears after a few days when you get stuck in to playing GAA and trying to shift a few cailíní. Not so bad!

Some positives about going to the Gaeltacht:

- making new friends who you promise to stay in contact with but who you never hear from again after you leave

- playing loads of GAA

- ceilí dancing, even if you make a hames of it at first and never manage to get over the walls of Limerick

- shifting at the disco on your last night.

Some negatives about going to the Gaeltacht:

- 🍀 Irish classes *every* day

- 🍀 getting in trouble for speaking English

- 🍀 your bean an tí being no craic and feeding you rotten food

- 🍀 not being much better at Irish when you leave, because you were more interested in shifting than in learning.

The Many Irish Accents

Ireland is a small country, as you know. Thirty-two counties, North and South, but the array of different accents is crazy. Ever witness a conversation between someone from Cork and Co. Donegal? You might as well be a man from Latvia having a chat with a bloke from Tokyo.

In Cork everything is high pitched and fast, 'Well, boiii.' In Co. Monaghan everything is slowed down. 'Well, how's things? I'm from Monnnaghan, hey!'

In Dublin you have the working-class accent, which can be intimidating – ''Mon, da Dubzzz!' –

but you also have the softly spoken and la-di-da – 'Can I get a cup of skinny latte, please?'

Up North in Co. Tyrone you have the quick accent. 'Ah, Peter Canavan was the greatest forward of all time, only he's not from Kerry!'

Most counties even have their own sayings and slang. Here's a situation for you that demonstrates the variety of accents in Ireland and how it can change dramatically if you go twenty miles down the road. A man was asked to clean out a garage for €50, but he wasn't too happy about the offer. This is how some of the counties would explain what happened in their own way:

Dublin. Here, wait till I tell ya about this bleedin' pox. The dope was on to me about cleaning out his garage for fifty bob. I told him to go an' ask me bollox . . .

Cork. Here, boi, would you believe some langer asked me to clear out his garage for €50? What aaa tool!

Donegal. Well, sir, this wee fella asked me to clean out his garage for €50. I swear, I . . . I . . . I . . .

Galway. Whisssth till I tell you. T''is man asssk me to clear out his garage for €50. I told him to head off and have a shite for himself.

Cavan. Can you believe that a man asked me to clean out his garage and offered me €50 for it? It was the happiest day of my life. I asked him, if he has any other garages to clear out, to ring me and nobody else!

Irish Slang

Most of our lives we use words and sayings that nobody but the Irish people will understand.

- You will in your bollox
  You won't be doing that

- Yeah, good one!
  You're telling lies

- Grand stretch in the evenings
  The weather is getting brighter every day

- The head on that fella
  He's funny-looking

- I will, yeah
  There's no chance I'm doing that

- Any auld craic with ya?
  Have you any news?

- Jesus, I'm dying
  I had too much to drink last night

☘ Go on away out of that
I don't believe you one bit

☘ Sure look it
I have nothing left to say to you, so please go away

☘ Sure we'll do it for the craic
It could be life-threatening, but as long as we can knock a bit of fun out of it it'll be worth doing.

The word 'grand'

Without doubt, this it the most frequent word to come out of the Irish voice box.

If you have no English and want to survive in Ireland, you need to know this one word, because it covers just about everything.

☘ How are you feeling today? *Grand.*

☘ Is it okay if I give you back that €100 next week? *Grand.*

☘ How is Tommy keeping after that bad fall? *Ah, he's grand.*

☘ Did ya enjoy your dinner? *It was grand.*

🍀 How did ya get on at the interview. *Ah, grand.*

🍀 Would ya mind doing that for me when you get the chance? *Yeah, grand.*

This word is so versatile that you can use it if you're happy, if you're sad, if you're excited, if you're hungover, if you're fresh.

Afterword: Understanding Mental Health

Even though this book was intended to give you a laugh and remind you again of how similar we Irish people are – which I hope it has! – I also wanted to add something about mental health. As those of you who have been following me for the last few years will know, this subject is something I'm very passionate about.

I try to look at everything from a simple point of view. I always have, and I try to do the same for mental health. For some reason our nation has attached a stigma to mental health. I'm only learning and understanding more and more about it as I get older.

Suicide, as you know, is a major problem in Ireland, and it has been for a long time. Is the issue being tackled enough from the top table? Absolutely not. I believe that there have been some improvements, but much more can be done by us in relation to this devastating phenomenon.

I don't care what anyone says: at some point in your life you'll experience depression. Some will suffer from a severe form in which you struggle for days at a time to leave the bed, and others might be lucky in suffering only a mild form of it. By mild I mean that you'll have a sort of cloud over you for a couple of days, and you won't be able to figure out what's wrong with you. 'My life is good at the minute. Things are going well, but I don't feel myself at all.' This is perfectly normal, and the only way to meet it head on is by talking about it to a friend or family member. You'll be amazed how much better you'll feel once you get the thoughts out of your head and throw them down on the table in front of someone. They say that one of the hardest things to do is to open up about feeling this way, but it is very rewarding mentally once you do.

Young men, especially, struggle with this problem. They see it as 'weak', 'soft' or 'cowardly' to admit that they're suffering a mental health issue. But this cannot be further from the truth: it is an extremely brave thing to admit to, because it means putting your hand up and saying, 'I'm not in a good place here.'

The amazing thing about depression is that it can often affect the people we least suspect. How many times have you heard, after someone has taken their life, 'God, I cannot believe that of him. He was always the life and soul of the party. He must have been suffering terribly inside.'

You see, for some reason it's not always the fella who looks depressed in the pub, sitting in the corner and staring into his pint: it's often the fella who's up on the dancefloor giving it welly that you need to be most worried about. This is especially true if it is out of character for them, because studies suggest that when a person has given in to the demons of depression, and has decided that they're going to take their own life, they're in seemingly good form leading up to it. It's as if they've been choked for the past while and, now that they've given in, the grip around their throat has been released and they're now at peace. It's a frightening thought, but it is a fact.

How can we, as a nation, come to grips with the problem? Well, it starts with number 1: minding yourself!

As you know, and as I have shown throughout this book, alcohol is a massive part of Irish culture. But such an intake of drink can often be a trigger for mental health problems. I'm speaking from my own experience, and I have no problem admitting that I suffer from depression now and again.

But I manage as best I can. Regular exercise and eating well are crucial. I can't emphasise enough how much of a 'free drug' exercise is for the brain. It's the most powerful drug on offer – trust me on this one.

I have often said to friends that if you're not in a good place mentally, the first thing to do is to go off drink or any other substance that might be affecting your outlook. Then you should start exercising three to four times a week. Doing these things will cure many of your demons.

Christmas is the time of year when you need to look out for each other the most, because, as we know from the amount of drinking that goes on, there will be plenty of negative thoughts racing through your mind. I enjoy a few pints as much as the next thirsty fella mad for craic; but the older I get, the more I've become aware of the effects of this way of life. You almost need to be mentally ready for it.

For example, you go on a two-day bender for a stag party, and you know that you're in for two or three days of mental torture after it, with nothing but demons and negative thoughts racing through your mind. What gets me through this is knowing that it's just the drink playing tricks on me and that it will pass.

This is important to know, because the 'beer fear' can often hammer your depression button, and, as anyone can tell you, it makes for a very tough few days with your own thoughts. So the next time you're lying in bed at three in the morning, with the imaginary rats running round your room, just remember that this will pass and that everything will be fine again once the drink has left your system.

I can tell you that the majority of people, especially men, who approach me with a few drinks on them on a night out do so not to praise my comedy skits but to thank me for the few videos I've made about depression and mental health. They say these videos have helped them understand the subject, and some of them have asked for help after recognising themselves in my videos, seeing themselves as suffering deep down.

That gives me a better feeling than any praise a funny video could ever get, knowing that I might just have helped a suffering person in even a small way.

So, *always* remember, folks: it's okay not to feel okay, and it's absolutely okay to ask for help.

Mind yourself!